空手道

全日本空手道連盟和道会

名誉会長　最高師範

大塚博紀著

All Japan Karate League - WadoKai
Honorable Chairman - Supreme Instructor
Otsuka Hironori - Author

WADO RYU KARATE

by Hironori Otsuka

translated by
Shingo Ishida

editor in charge of layout
Annette Hellingrath

photo reproductions by
Dale Housser

ISBN 0-920129-18-8
First Printing 1997

PRINTED IN HONG KONG

MASTERS PUBLICATION
Hamilton ● Ontario ● Canada

私の言葉

My Words

In the 25th year of the Showa era, I responded to the Wadokai's passion towards karate by printing 1500 copies of "Studying Karate Kata, Part 1" and giving them to a group of Wadokai members.

I am clumsy with writing skillfully; thus, I am reluctant to hold a pencil. I was able to author the small work above with assistance from Tetsuga Ojima and Tetsuro Shibaya, First Captain and Second Captain respectively, of the Karate Club at the University of Tokyo at the time the books were printed.

As with other martial arts, progress in skill can not come from training with the instructor (shidoshi) alone. Training by one's self with only a written text could only be more difficult. There is no other way to progress except to study under a good instructor and years of effort.

I, myself, find difficulty in putting into written text what I have difficulty in expressing with speech. With consideration to this fact, I found myself reluctant to publish the above work, with my added clumsiness at writing skillfully. This work is a re-organization of some material I had gathered over the past years. This was to be published on my birthday, June 1st but was unfortunately late coming to press. I was attending to some personal and public duties, in addition to the fact that I was instructing for approximately 3 1/2 months in both Europe and America.

From now on, if other books are to be published I intend to place all my efforts into its completion, as quickly as possible. I intend to follow this work with other works on kata, fundamentals of kumite-kata, variations of certain kata, women's self defense skills, skills for law enforcement officers, etc. These works will be based upon my own, personal conversations and study, hence, there may be some imperfections which I believe will be present, especially with regards to how I express these works. If my works, no matter how insignificant, can help any readers, nothing would please me more.

I would also like to gratefully acknowledge the assistance from three men who helped me to get this work completed: Heiji Maizumi, a graduate from the karate club at the Japanese University of Dentistry; Toei Arimoto, coach of the same as above, and Kinsei Yamada, a graduate from the Karate Club of the University of Kyoto.

- 44th Year of the Showa Era, Autumn
Hironori Otsuka

昭和44年　晩秋

大 塚 博 紀

Post-script

I was to have completed this book for publishing by autumn of the 44th year of the Showa era. However, with my duties and commitments to others, the year had passed.

I departed Japan from Haneda airport on February 3rd because it was suddenly decided that the Wadokai in London would participate in the all-European contest on February 27th. With this sudden departure, I was requested to leave some form of an organized work to be published, when in fact, it was not ready.

I handed what I had quickly organized to Kinsei Yamada, who, by March 29th, had re-organized everything I handed to him before my departure. Needless to say, I was surprised and thankful at the same time, to him and all those individuals who made this publishing possible. I immediately put myself to re-read this work and check for any errors, but, with my tendency to procrastinate, I thought it would be better to publish it, as is, in its fine form and place more effort on my next work to follow. I hereby gratefully acknowledge the efforts of all those involved in the completion of this work and apologize for my tardiness which hindered the completion of this work.

- May, 45th Year of the Showa Era,
The Author

Contents

師 範 武 歴

Martial Chronology of the Instructor

June 1st, 1892 *-Born in Ibaragi prefecture.*

April, 1898 *-Begins training of jui-jitsu.*

Spring, 1911 *-Continues training in jui-jitsu, with special emphasis on Toshin-kenpo.*

June 1st, 1921 *-Inherits the right to propagate Chin-style jui-jitsu from the third Master, Tasusaburo Nakayama.*

Spring, 1922 *-Begins training in karate; founds the Wado Ryu karate techniques by incorporating some techniques from the Japanese Kobudo.*

1929, onwards *-Studies how to make karate competition possible; forms the fundamental rules for present-day competitions and contests.*

Autumn, 1934 *-Establishes Wadokai in All-Japan Karate League, with almost 300 locations in the present. Locations in Universities, prefectural government offices, companies and overseas (Europe and America) locations.*

April 29, 1966 *-Recipient of Soko Asahi Award for dedication to karate.*

Current responsibilities *-All Japan Karate League - Wadokai, honourable chairman, Supreme Instructor.*
-All Japan Karate League - Vice Chairman.
-Director, Japan Kobudo Association.

師範語録

Analects of the Instructor

武の道は　たゞあら事と　な思ひそ
和の道究め　和を求む道

博紀

'The way of the martial arts is not an ordinary thing.
It is to master peace and to desire harmony.'

Hironori Otsuka

武 道 の 発 祥

The Origin of Martial Arts

I do not possess very specific knowledge of history - thus, I can not accurately state the historical origin of the martial arts. However, I believe that the following may be possible. Almost all animals possess some sort of ability or thing with which to protect themselves from external harm. These include camouflage, poison, accurate vision, fangs, claws, horns, swift movement and agility, flight and others, to name a few. Each also has their own, particular method with which to fight.

Humans, also, have this ability to fight although this ability varies greatly from person to person. Methods for punching, kicking and throwing exist as habits for some individuals.

Human beings may have incorporated this natural ability to hunt for food, or to protect themselves from their prey. Then this ability to fight was used by the strong to control the weak, leading to the establishment of organized groups and associations. In order to not only maintain the unity and stability of this group, power was required in order to maintain the group's authority over others.

Along with the development of society, weapons and arms were created along with their methods of usage and born was the sword, the bow and arrow and the gun. Also, methods of fighting that did not incorporate weapons such as: sumo, jui-jitsu and karate developed further. Scientific progress now reached points where the hydrogen bomb and nuclear missiles were easily produced.

For as long as humans possessed greed and desire, this conclusion was inevitable. Needless to say, in prehistoric times, this was not the case - it was more peaceful. The irony in scientific progress is that by making people's lives easier to live, it has disrupted the order and peace that previously existed in society. There is no end to scientific progress. Weapons development will eventually, if it has not already, reach a point where weapons will only serve to destroy ourselves. This then, would make humans no different from primitive beasts. Hence, the establishment of martial arts begins to serve its purpose.

武　の　道

The Path of Martial Arts

It is said that chivalry / military affairs symbolizes peace. The character / ideogram for military affairs divides into two parts, one to mean warfare or fighting, while the other part means to lessen. An old saying states, "lessen warfare and conflict in the world to establish peace and make life fruitful." Thus, this statement is essentially the meaning of the character / ideogram of military affairs and this is the path of martial arts.

All nations and societies adapt their main beliefs according to time and progressional change. Chivalry similarly adapts itself and re-directs itself as well, of course. In feudal times, the only objective of concern was to be victorious over the enemy - emphasis was placed on skill, practice and strength of the body.

After the wars, during the peaceful, re-constructing of society, focus was shifted, to be placed upon mental strengths such as loyalty, integrity, sacrifice and dedication. From the Tokugawa era onwards, such shifts of focus and emphasis occurred not only in the military class, but for the ordinary, everyday citizens as well.

So, chivalry returned to its emphasis on peace - however, it was used as a method with which to maintain authority of control by certain individuals. As history progressed to the Maiji, Taisho, Showa eras and as we saw the eventual defeat of Japan in World War 2, chivalry maintained its existence in society in one form or another.

Then, we saw the birth of a democratic nation in Japan from its previous, fascist state. Peace and harmony for such a highly progressive and culturally developmental society must not be for one individual nor one government. It must be peace for every individual. If this is not so, peace and true happiness can never occur for neither the nation or its constituent individuals.

The path of martial arts is the path for peace. By mastering the path of martial arts, which is the path of peace and desiring the path of peace consequently, is indeed the true path of the martial arts. The essence of the path of martial arts lies in the peace and happiness of all human beings. Regardless of the change that time brings; as it was in the past, martial arts has not altered its true essence now and it never will, in the future to come.

道　と　術

The Path and Technique

In the past, ken-jitsu, jui-jitsu and archery, etc. were called techniques. During the Meiji era, the late Jigoro Kano began to call jui-jitsu "judo," ken-jitsu "kendo," and so on; incorporating "path" into the name instead of technique.

There was an inclination however, during the Meiji era to downplay the value of martial arts due to the cultural expansion of Japanese society. Equality was emphasized, thus, martial arts were no longer exclusive to the feudal class and peasants, farmers - "normal" people - were free to practice martial arts.

The feudal class too, began to practice other forms of martial arts as well, due to no longer being exclusive - martial arts became unimportant to a certain extent. Later on however, interest in the martial arts was re-established as kendo and judo became incorporated with physical education at schools and other educational institutions.

How then, is "path" and "technique" different? Looking at the characters for both, they both intend some type of logic.

"Path" and "technique" intend the same objective. There is no difference in using either term. During the Meiji era, it may seem to have sounded more prideful or "established" to use "path" rather than "technique." This may be so because "path" seems to emphasize the mental aspect more than just the technique by itself. If that is the case, then, there is a difference between "path" and "technique."

The relationship between techniques and the mental aspects of martial art disappears and would not lead to one's mastering of that martial art. "Technique" is said to include both the mind and skill. Therefore then, "path" ought to be defined similarly.

To regard with the view that skill is inferior to the mind in importance would be utterly pointless and futile. In order to address both skill and the mind, it should not matter whether "path" or "technique" is used. If "path" sounds more correct, that is fine; however, no bias should be placed on "technique."

Conversely, the same applies for "technique," as well. To see this situation otherwise would be synonymous with blasphemy of the martial arts itself. Skill must be the kind of skill that expresses the mind. By practicing with skill that expresses one's mind can one train his own mind. The mind and skill of martial arts must be one unified whole, or there would be no meaning to training for that martial art. A lack of that unity as one would be detrimental to society; if such is the case, martial arts should not even be practiced or learned.

武技鍛錬の目的

The Purpose of Training for Martial Arts

Every person thinks differently for themselves.

There are those who seek to strengthen their mind, those who seek to strengthen the body, those who seek a method of self defense, those who require martial arts due to their occupation, those who have an interest in it leisurely, those who may have a combination of the above, or just other reasons why.

It is inevitably true that each person has his own objectives for training in the martial arts. However, those who learn and those who instruct must act with the notion of learning the true essence of that martial art. For many, if they do not believe in the above to begin with, they will see that as time progresses, a feeling of "incompleteness" will become apparent and hold true. Eventually, this incomplete feeling begins to affect the mind as well. This is the point at which one's character becomes essential.

However, if one's objective is to improve his mind and character there must be numerous methods other than martial arts to do so. Similarly, if one's objective is for the body, there must be other methods as well. Correct mental training is extremely difficult. To surpass this discrepancy, training that allows one to compete by matching strength to strength, body to body with another person is very effective. However, the strictness of such a competitive form of training, unfortunately, is similar to a violent, effective medicine.

If a correct method is utilized in application, amazing benefits will result; however, if incorrect, grave damage may result as well. Those who seek to train their mind must keep in perspective of their goals; by not being led astray towards evil, while simultaneously requiring the strict, but righteous teaching from the instructor and friendship and support from his fellow students.

To learn any martial art, one must constantly bear in his mind both intelligence and wisdom. He must possess a strong, endurable mental strength as well as the physical ability in equal proportion, in order to not quit his training before it is complete. Therefore, the objective of martial arts training is to train and improve the "path" of the martial arts mentality of an individual.

武道精神とは何か

What is the Mentality of the Path of Martial Arts?

Peace, as the root essence of martial art, is easy to say in word, but it is not as easy in action or as reality in human society. By looking at past history and the current state of international affairs, one might even say that it is impossible.

However, no matter how impossible it seems, if peace does not exist in society, human existence will never be happy or prosperous. No matter how difficult or impossible it may seem, peace must occur. God, Buddha or other entities will not bring it to us. Human beings must establish peace on their own. Human society, having progressed from a simple, feudalistic state to its current, complex, scientific state, makes this task even more difficult for itself.

Human beings will require extraordinary mental powers to accomplish this seemingly impossible task. This "extraordinary mental power" is the mentality of the martial arts. Such a mentality will be a powerful driving force in the attempt to bring peace and order to humanity. The mentality of the martial arts is the required, extraordinary ability to achieve this difficult, if not impossible objective for all human beings.

武道精神は現代人にも必要

Martial Arts Mentality - Necessary for Present Day People

It is unfortunate and regrettable that "martial arts mentality" sounds so feudal and contrary to contemporary society. This is probably the result of martial art forms being utilized by certain individuals during the feudal eras to oppress people, as well as the ignorance of the general population.

With the end of World War 2 and its consequent democracy in Japanese society, words such as "feudalism" and any notions associated with it may seem unattractive. As stated before, the "path" of the martial arts is the foundation of a peaceful society and exists to better the collective existence of humanity; thus, it is unconditionally necessary - the person who walks this "path" has to see that it is indeed necessary regardless of date and time.

Developments in communication and transportation "lessens" the distance from nation to nation, creating friction, doubt and conflict between people. Establishment of peace then, likely is to increase in difficulty as time progresses. Therefore, the martial arts mentality becomes increasingly necessary. Essentially, what is most important is to be able to use this appropriately within the limits of society.

文武両道は不離不即

Words and Actions are Never Separated from Each Other

The difficult task of establishing peace can not be accomplished with the martial arts mentality alone. What exactly is peace?

Questions such as how to bring such peace about into society can not even begin to be answered by ordinary, everyday individuals like myself. Politics, economics, science, education, religion, rationality, philosophy, fine arts, etc., all play a part undoubtedly. More than likely, it would be a combination of one or more of the above to reach a solution that can be true.

However, even if this consensus is reached, the idea on its own will not bring peace. In order to actualize the idea, a powerful, driving force would become necessary. In other words, the ability to perform decisive actions. The martial arts mentality is the ability to bring peace and order. One can not be interrupted by obstructions on his path towards what is right; he must strive and possess the ability to actualize his objectives. But decisive action alone will involve danger.

It is obvious that one must combine independence with reason and high admirable ideals when performing whatever action he performs. Also, high knowledge must be achieved through high levels of education. Also, to be able to utilize the knowledge gained through high levels of education. Also, to be able to utilize the knowledge gained through words and grammar is also a strength of the martial arts mentality. High levels of grammatical and semantic ability are what allows one to properly and effectively realize or exhibit the martial arts mentality. Regardless of how high one's martial grammatical abilities are, if both components are not equal in proportion to each other, grave, disastrous harm may result. Hence words and action, like wings to a bird, are never separate from each other.

現代武道の在り方

How Martial Arts Exist in the Present

The fact that peace is the true essence of military affairs, has been, is and will always be, unchanged. But how it exists varies depending upon the chronological setting and progress of time.

Therefore, present martial arts must account for this fact in its presence and make their prime objective the cultivation of human beings· who possess high intellectual ability, good emotional control, as well as a healthy mind and body. These qualities and their strife towards them must not be enforced upon them. Rather, individuals must self-realize that it is their responsibility, as a part of a democratic society such as ours. It can never be a feudal martial art that ignores independence and rationality.

Also, it must be understood that it is not for personal gain or benefit, but for peace and social order - to improve the lives of everyone in society. In can not be a "path" separate from society; it must be a "path" for the society in question.

Present martial arts must be virtuous. It can not become strictly for competitive purposes only, either. History dictates that once virtue disappears, martial arts would only become "poisonous" to society. Martial arts in the present must place peace and welfare of the society as its objective.

武道精神と武技鍛錬との関連性

The Relationship Between Martial Arts Training-Martial Arts Mentality

Training for martial arts in the present occurs by utilizing life-and-death techniques under conditions which must completely protect one from danger.

When training, one must never forget the seriousness of the actions he is performing. Training should allow one to quickly and accurately observe the opponents's posture or action, swiftly and correctly judge the environment surrounding him and quickly respond appropriately to his situation. There can not be even a single moment of hesitation or reluctance.

With passing time, one will develop his ability to respond, his judgment ability and ability to execute actions. Also, martial arts is said to "begin with a bow and end with a bow" emphasis is placed upon one's courtesy. This courtesy in martial arts is an expression of respect for one's opponent. This respect then, is born from love. The courtesy to be expressed can not merely be "movement," rather, it must be a proper expression of respect out of love.

In order to express courtesy in martial arts properly, the bow itself must be perfect in the sense that one must be able to revert to an offensive or defensive stance regardless of whatever may occur as he is bowing. This is why bowing in martial arts differs from normal bowing; and it is with this awareness that one may train his mental abilities in martial arts.

When training in martial arts, if courtesy is lost, evil comes into consideration. One of the primary things while training in martial arts is the fact that bowing is an expression of respect out of love. One who trains under the instructor must constantly be aware of this fact, while the instructor must judge his student's ability, talent, strength, etc. and instruct accordingly with kindness, yet strictly.

Those who are learning, in turn, must support each other with friendship and a sense of togetherness. It is with this type of emotional contact over long periods of time that one cultivates his emotional control and moral nature. It must be emphasized that bowing comes from respect and that respect is born from love. Human beings love themselves the most, before others can be loved.

However, in order to truly love one's self, then, one must love society and all humanity living in that society. Those who love society will, in turn, be loved by that society and all humanity living in it. By loving others, the society and all humanity, one then truly loves himself. Both love each other, respect each other and finally, courtesy occurs. Humans also seek to become satisfied by fulfilling their respective desires. The pursuing of these desires is human life. That desire probably, is to wish that one is happy and content. How "contentedness" is thought of, or how it is received emotionally varies from person to person, but that "contentedness" must, of course, be proper.

Human beings can not exist alone. Together with others, they form society - and function only becomes possible when he is considered as a member of that group. Thus, if that society is not content, one can not have true contentedness for himself.

True contentedness can only be permitted to exist in a peaceful society. Only in a peaceful society can a virtuous, free and satisfying human existence occur. Respect and then love, gives birth to peace between people. Respect and love together makes one peaceful, then others, then society, which is then followed by all humanity. This peace is the true objective and wish of martial arts. The reason why martial arts begins and ends with a bow and so much emphasis is placed upon bowing is this; it is this desire for peace. Also, training in conditions of extreme cold or extreme heat over long periods of time, as well as physically stressful training will assist in gaining the mental (as well as physical) strength that can encounter any dire situation.

Developed judgement ability, increased moral strength and emotional control, trained mental and physical strength; all become the motivational factor and driving force of the peace that martial arts so longingly desires to achieve. Martial arts training is for the development and training of the martial arts mentality, which then is the driving force for peace.

武技は和の術

Martial Arts are Techniques for Peace

Martial arts and its techniques are for peace. The techniques are a form of peace being expressed through action. By training in such techniques, one observes the ideology behind martial arts - as well as developing the mentality to observe peace.

Being an expression of peace, martial arts have no impossibilities. It is both scientific and theoretical. It does not exceed heaven, it does not oppose the earth, it does not oppose people; it is in accord with all of these. Like the blowing wind and the flowing water, it is in accord with the ways of nature. Water always flows from high to low. When the flow is obstructed, water goes around this obstruction and continues to flow smoothly as before. It will flow through the smallest of spaces and cracks, perhaps taking along with its flow anything that stands in its way.

Likewise for the wind. A bottle gourd that floats on this flow of water rides above this invincible flow; hence, it never sinks.

The special terminology used to describe techniques in Japanese martial arts are truly an expression of peace and harmony. It is to not oppose an opponent's strong attack, but to use his strength and protect one's self from it, using the strength from that self-defense to attack the opponent in return. A waterwheel does not oppose the flow of water falling onto it; instead, using that strength, it works that strength to its advantage.

Likewise for a windmill - defense and offence both are in accord with the ways of nature. Defense and offence in martial arts work with the ways of nature. One's movements must be like a ball's -

uninterrupted and fluid. A ball's movement is smooth - it does not contradict or oppose the ways of nature. Techniques of martial arts must be flexible to change and other forces - like a "ball of air." Regardless of the degree of smoothness, a flow of movements must occur. A "ball of air" would move freely; from other external forces, it moves in accordance to its environment. It can change its shape and form infinitely. Thus, its surfaces and limits change infinitely. There is shape without shape, surface without surface and limit without limit. These changes are infinite. Like outer space, it is infinitely limitless. It is like the sky. This infinity embraces all things and makes peace. In martial arts, there is no such thing as the ultimate technique. Techniques must be infinitely changeable and altered - just like the sky and space.

The form and shape of martial arts form the "entrance" into infinity and limitlessness. Limitless forms and unshaped techniques make martial arts. And therefore, it is the technique of peace. By training the forms and techniques which express peace, one walks along the "path" of peace which is the objective of martial arts, which then allows one to develop the mentality for peace. Thus, if the technique is not in the interests of peace, it is not a martial art. Actually, this would then defy nature and instead bring calamity - peace would be lost.

Techniques of martial art is not just a pattern of movement - it is the form of peace expressed through and in accordance with, the ways of nature, heaven, earth and people.

正 拳

"Sei Ken"
(Righteousness of the Fist)

If one's heart is not righteous, neither is his sword. The sword is said to be the soul of a swordsman; hence, to properly study the way of the sword, one must have a righteous heart to do so as well. The essence of karate, the fist, is no different. If one's heart is not righteous, he risks the dangers of misuse and any resulting evil. "To have a righteous heart" sounds easy, however, humans are often tempted by evil in every aspect of life - thus, in fact, it is very difficult to possess a "righteous heart."

By correctly training in a martial art, one is able to correctly train his heart as well. Hence, the martial art being trained for must be correct in every conceivable aspect. The martial art can not be said to be "correct" unless it is in harmony with the logic and reason of both heaven and earth. The "righteous" fist is that of "peace" and a "righteous" heart is that of "peace."

The righteous path of the fist, therefore, is a path of peace.

理想と現実

The Ideal and the Reality

Is is possible, then, to actualize this "righteous" path of the martial arts? Due to the never-ending differences in politics, economics and other differences of the human race, this actualization would encounter many difficulties. Besides, no humans have identical ideals or beliefs. There will always be differences between a nation and its nationals. There could be situations where these beliefs disagree with each other and result in an inevitable clash of individuals.

There will always be differences in one's personal history, religion, habits, education and so on. Can peace and social harmony be maintained with all these differences? There will always be an inevitable clash of opinions and beliefs - always.

Even today, differences exist that separate individuals from each other. The strong oppress the weak - an undeniable reality and it is very difficult to achieve peace and harmony for everyone. This is why, since ancient times, there have been stories of messiahs, angels, apocalypses and births of religious sects all over the world. Those mentioned above are similar to medicines which only provide temporary relief for terminal diseases.

武道精神とスポーツ精神

Martial Arts Mentality and the "Sports" Mentality

Peace for mankind may be like providing a cure for a terminal disease. It may be a terminal disease, but is it correct to just give up? Similarly, is it correct to allow the strong to oppress the weak; to allow a small number of individuals gain to the loss of a larger whole? The fact that one thinks "no, something must be done" is also reality. By leaving this problem alone, its inevitable result - the wilting death of nations and individuals - is more than clear.

When humans see that they are about to die, they would attempt any action possible to not die. But is it a part of human nature that, albeit slowly, we are all, in fact, dying and yet we are able to live normally from day to day? If we are all gradually dying, then peace seems to be impossible. Unless every human being becomes a buddha, a shaka, or Jesus Christ, peace for humanity seems impossible. We, however, obviously do not desire this result.

Every individual must place effort into actions which will better himself both mentally and physically. By increasing the number of such individuals, we increase the chances of achieving peace for humanity. Is martial arts not an appropriate instructor for such human improvement? But in modern society, it is difficult to dedicate one's self to the training of martial arts. Nowadays, it is difficult to even dedicate one's self to the improvement of his own self, let alone martial arts. It is a regrettable fact that there are individuals who, literally, sell martial arts for his own gain and not to improve himself or others. In turn, this action is like spilling poison into a river; it only serves to harm society. Peace is a matter which all human beings must think about. For humankind to desire peace is most important, yet it is also most difficult. To make this tenuous ideal come even one step closer to reality is the task of all human beings.

I have very little knowledge of human physical education. However, I doubt that sports is only to increase physical strength; it is also to develop both mentally and physically.

Through action, the development of mind, intellect, judgment and so on to produce a "better" human individual must be the same as in training for a martial art. The ultimate objective, to produce peace and harmony, is not any different from the objective of martial arts training. Of course, there should be no difference. To deter from this essential fact and become a "glamorous" athlete, or to use one's own athletic abilities for his own, personal gain, is to invite his inevitable downfall. Sport by itself is harmful. Thus, I believe firmly that the "sports" mentality and the "martial arts mentality" are one and the same; with identical objectives and goals.

妥協と協調

Compromise and Co-operation

Power and compromise should not be used to solve every problem, every time. There will always be disagreement as one tries to argue based on ideals rather than history or fact. One must converse patiently - never hurriedly. There will be times when, even conversing patiently, that an agreeable resolution will not emerge. However, if any agreement or consensus can be identified, opposing sides will come that much closer to a resolution.

If the parties approach each other, they will eventually overlap. It does not matter if it happens in one year or ten years. The mentality to approach one's own ideals, however, is intolerable. Since it is easier to solve a problem through the use of power or might, humans often tend to exercise such things.

Those things obtained through power and might will, eventually be lost through other's power and might. A glance at our own history, China's history, or Western Europe's history proves this. The shogun Hideyoshi ruled for only 30 days! However, his successor, Tokugawa, made his dynasty last almost 260 years. This is most likely because Tokugawa utilized government and politics, instead of military might, with which to rule the land. Power and compromise always root evil. Co-operation (and understanding) takes precedence in anything.

守　破　離

Shuhari

In martial arts, there is a word - "Shuhari" - that has always existed. It also seems to exist in Japanese tea ceremonies and I do not know from which this word was born.

"Shu" means to maintain the teachings of the predecessor and strict adherence to them; "ha" is to doubt anything that serves to disrupt that action. "Ri" is to be separated from the first two and improve on the teachings whenever possible. This not only applies to martial arts, but

other disciplines as well. However, it is difficult to actually master any teaching - never less than five or ten years and varies upon the natural ability of the individual.

Besides, even if one is talented, serious training requires a lack of food or sleep sometimes - some things not possible for people in modern society. It is redeeming, however, to see that certain groups and organizations have recognized and honored those individuals who engage in "Shuhari" in whatever disciplines they maintain.

武道道場祭神への拝礼

The Worship of the Martial Arts Dojo

Since ancient times, as a matter of habit, dojos have all had some kind of gods enshrined inside them. It was usually the god in which the owner of the dojo believed.

After World War 2, the occupying forces had forbidden martial arts in the police and public schools. Later, martial arts were permitted, but martial arts and religion were separated from each other. Hence, many dojos existed without small enshrinements for individual gods. Nowadays, some places have small enshrinements, but this is only a decoration. Or else, some decorate their dojos with names of recognized individuals and not miniature enshrinements.

There are some dojos that practice proper bowing and so on entry / exit or start / end of training (as in before WW2), whereas some others do not observe bowing and so on, or become basketball courts, a place for children to play and so on.

After WW2, some believed it was unnecessary to bow or show proper respect when entering a dojo because martial arts and religion were separated.

However, currently, this is not so: people decorate with proper enshrinements or observe proper bowing and so on.

Nevertheless, it is still very summarily done or improper. The young nowadays do not believe in the gods. If one can pray to god and improve his skills, no one would go through the effort of training. And it is not just a matter of habit. Training for martial arts is in order for one to improve himself as a proper member of society. The dojo in which this training is done is nothing short of sacred. Thus, any shortcomings of respect with dojos are not tolerable. However, humans naturally have a weak side to themselves. They become upset or angry while training inside the dojo. One can not become emotional every time - one can not train properly if this is so. Martial arts would then become wasteful.

There are ten "evils" in training for martial arts. These ten "evils" never leave one alone. To rid one's self of these things and train for himself is not an easy task. To ask for help from his god does not help things. One must oppress his weakness by himself. When one finds his weakness while training to improve himself, it is then that his god will observe and protect him from that weakness. One must do this responsibly.

If one has no god, then the same effect can be obtained from one's parents. It is fine to ask one's parents for help. It is possible to repay one's parents somehow after one's training is completed. Those individuals whose parents have passed may use the spirit of the deceased.

Or one can ask his own self for support. It does not matter to whom or what one clings for help; it is how he clings. Bowing is not just form, it is an expression of one's soul. Pray to one's own heart - it does not matter how help is achieved. "To respect god and yet not depend on him" - these are the words of Eiji Yoshikama, a famous author. Indeed, these words are words to remember.

形に入って形から抜ける

Enter into Kata, then Withdraw from Kata

The martial arts have numerous varieties of kata. Predecessors, over long periods of time, created kata through experience, changes and imagination.

It is obvious that these kata must be trained and practiced sufficiently, but one must not be "stuck" in them. One must withdraw from kata to produce forms with no limits or else it becomes useless. It is important to alter the form of the trained kata without hesitation to produce countless other forms by training. Essentially, it is a habit - created over long periods of training. Because it is a habit, it comes to life with no hesitation - by the subconscious mind. These habits occur without one realizing it, so one sometimes does not even notice.

The point to be careful about such habits is that these habits may still emerge in situations where they are inappropriate, or even dangerous, to emerge. It is difficult to rid one's self of such habits. "Look at other's mistakes to correct yourself" - an old saying, but how true!

Like an actor who is able to portray different characters, martial arts ought to be the same. To not have it happen consciously, but as a matter of habit, yet a habit not so entrenched to cause negative effects - not an easy task. Martial arts training has no end. This is because one can never stop training.

型　と　形

Igata and Kata

The first character, is read as "igata." Pots made from the igata of pots are all the same, with no differences. Igata of pots serve no other purpose, except to make pots.

Martial arts must never become an "igata." It is always "kata." "Kata" is to express; as a mirror does, it changes with every action and situation. A mirror figure changes just as its reflection does. This, essentially, is the "kata" of martial arts.

"Igata" is dead - it has no life; "kata" is alive. The dead "igata" has no purpose. Because kata is alive, it can be utilized. Thus, when using the kata of martial arts, one must use it in accordance to the meaning and objective it has, or else it becomes useless.

To use an alive kata is difficult, but it is important in martial arts training. Depending on the individual using it, the same kata can be very different. This is because one's personality shows through in his kata. The fact that "kata" is preferred over "igata" does not apply only to martial arts alone. In writing, if one writes in an "igata" manner, the words do not "live" - it only becomes a sign or display of words. It may seem wonderful, but looks alone can not be said to be skillful.

In order to excel in writing, one must practice at least three years, I heard. Otherwise, words will "die." The same can be said for indigenous folk dancing. The manner in which one moves his body, arms, legs may appear to be beautiful, ("igata") but if the dance itself ("kata") is dead, the dancing becomes meaningless. The music, lyrics, dance and so on first come to "life" only when it is kata and not igata, are observed. Acting, music, singing - all are applicable.

When unrelated igata is combined to music, dance, or song (or anything else), it becomes meaningless. In martial arts, the movements in each kata are no exception. These movements are identical to the stroke of the brush in writing.

Correct movements, together as a whole, form the fundamental movements which form the kata. Kata must be correct, unlimited and most of all, alive. Martial arts progresses from kata to kumite, kumite to combat and so on. Kata is a fundamental aspect of martial arts and hence is unyieldingly important. It can never just be "form." It is essential to train for the "living" form. Martial arts, then is a "kata" - not an "igata."

大きい業と無駄な業の相違

The Difference Between Large and Excessive Actions

Each movement of the fundamental katas must be large and lively, but not excessive or pointless. From these larger movements, one progresses to faster movements. One must begin from fundamental movements to kata, to kumite, to changes in the kumite and to combat, or else he will not improve at all.

"Larger" movements mean, meaningful, lively movements, not pointless or excessive actions and motion of the hands and feet. Too much motion does not equal "large" movement. One often sees this in a contest, but when one wishes to punch as he is jumping in towards an opponent, he has the tendency to draw his fist backwards and to his side before he actually punches. This is because one attempts to punch on the strength of his arm alone - involving unnecessary motions as a result.

There is an inefficient distribution of power and thus, power is wasted. In the above situation, by punching with the strength of the arm alone, it contradicts the movement of the body. This can not be called a "large and lively" movement. It is a slow movement, with excessive motions. Hence, it is an improper punch since it ignores the fundamentals of punching an opponent. Any unnecessary motions before and after a punch just get in the way of a proper punch and is pointless.

Power is only necessary at the exact moment of contact. This not only applies to punches, but defenses as well. As stated earlier, there must be no limitations on one's movement. Using the "dead" igata form with which to punch involves unnecessary pointless action. This, in turn, serves to weaken the punch compared to its actual potential to hit the opponent.

These pointless actions and inefficient usage of power will begin to show themselves regularly. They are indeed, not large movements, but excessive and pointless actions. They can become habitual and serve to prevent one from improving his skills.

However, as stated earlier, there is no such thing as an end or finish to how well a kata training can be done. "Good" or "bad" is subjective - hence you are "good" or "bad" when compared to your opponent. Thus, depending on one's opponent, it may sometimes be advantageous to involve excessive action or motion. Excessive or pointless actions can also be a strategy.

速い業と細かい業の相違

The Difference Between Quick and Fine Actions

"Quick" action refers to action with no excessive movement and performed in the shortest amount of time possible; not actions of the hand or fingers (called "fine" actions), and is a correct derivative movement of karate's fundamental actions.

"Fine" actions seem quick, but are actually slow and not too strong, if not too effective. Of course, if it is advantageous to do so, one should use "fine" actions only. For example, "fine" actions include attacks to the opponent's eyes, throat, biting, scratching, or small stabs

with the elbow.

Also "quick" actions are not just "quick," but must have force and an objective for its usage as well.

武技と護身

Martial Technique and Self Defense

The lives and resources of citizens must be protected and maintained by the country, but in reality, one can only rely upon the powers of the law. Harm can result from a lack of caution being used by the individual, but one can suffer unprovoked, uncalled for harm. In some situations, a mastering of martial arts could prevent, or at least minimize the effects from such harm.

There is nothing wrong with the fact that martial arts may be involved. But in martial arts, one's mind and heart must constantly be prepared and this preparation is of utmost importance. A plentiful amount of attention and caution is just as necessary.

However, it should be remembered that martial arts may interfere with safety, or worse, call harm to one's self in certain situations. At a point of life or death, if one intends on relying upon martial arts, then it is more and more required the he pay attention and use extreme caution in order to not achieve that point in the first place. It is important to create one's confidence in his skills through training, however, to become arrogant and rely upon that skill is most dangerous.

There is nothing as unfortunate as finding one's self in a situation where he must utilize martial arts to protect himself. The objective of martial arts training is to train hard and yet search for a state where martial arts need not be used. Hence, one must seek the path of peace and desire that path as well.

気構え，心構え

Preparing the Mind, Preparing the Heart

Both are synonymous. As stated earlier, it is unfortunate if one finds himself in a situation where he must use his martial arts skills.

There is an old saying: "Leave one's yard and find seven enemies." No matter how skilled one is in the martial arts, he will find himself unprepared if encountered off-guard. Ideally, then, one should constantly be in a state of preparedness.

In the past, samurai often slept with their swords sticking outside of their mosquito nets hung around the beds. If an intruder cut the supporting cords to the mosquito net, one is helpless. With a part of the sleeping samurai's swords sticking out, he could easily remove or cut away at the mosquito net should an intruder be encountered.

I have forgotten the time and place; but there was a samurai who was very skilled with the sword. One night, he drank some rice wine at a friend's house and armed only with a lantern, went home. The next morning, a servant of the host asked: "Sir, you were drunk last night, but even if you were attacked, you would have been able to protect yourself, right?" and the samurai replied, "No, a samurai must never overdrink, lest he risk losing his life to some attackers."

That would be true for any person excepting those we encounter in stories and fiction.

Back then, when walking past someone, one would go left and approach passers-by on the right. This was because swords are drawn with the right hand; this practice can still be imagined today, as cars travel on the left side of the road in Japan.

To the left, one would only leave enough space to allow for his defense, walk quietly to hear noises around himself and watch passers-by from the corner of the eyes. One would walk around a corner leaving enough space to observe that no one was on the other side and when opening doors or dividers, take one step back to observe the room before entering.

One would often extend his clothing into the room before he himself actually entered. Thieves would often remove windows to enter, but did not right away, because there may have been a guard, etc. waiting to kill him on the other side.

When I was a child, in the 35th year of the Meiji era, there were still a lot of samurai in existence. Yoshio Suzuki, a 75 year old samurai whom I knew, would always watch me out of the corner of his eye and step quietly whenever we passed by each other on the street. I was about ten and obviously had no intentions to kill him, yet, for Suzuki, it was a matter of habit.

In television and movies, one often sees an individual sitting in front of a hibachi fireplace smoking a long pipe. This was actually a defensive position - in case an intruder appeared without warning, the pipe could be thrown at the intruder's face, a sword reached for and as the intruder struggles to retrieve himself, the sitting man can kill the intruder. Hibachis are purposefully built waist high. The pipe, the hibachi and all these things are only the elements of mind preparation.

Again, in television and movies one often sees yakuza and gamblers wearing their robes loosely tied with a loose knot or no knot at all. This is in case the police come to grab the gambler or yakuza from behind to arrest him - he can disrobe quickly and get away.

Back then, walking around half naked or being barefoot was normal. Although not admirable, these yakuza and gamblers protected themselves with short swords hidden inside their waist wraps. Small objects were placed around exits, entrances and windows, all in preparation to throw these things at one's enemies. To throw ashtrays filled with ashes, or to throw pots filled with boiling water - these were all in preparation to encountering one's enemy.

The smoking pipe mentioned above is usually held in front of the mouth, but in the older days, it was held firmly in one hand and pointed to the side, in order to not allow a sudden intruder to push the pipe down the smoker's throat.

When drinking tea out of tea cups, instead of placing the cup on one's palms, one would hold it from the side with the index finger on the inner surface of the cup. So, in case the cup is forced against his head suddenly, the cup can not make contact with the head.

Even in the present, modern society, a female living alone may consider how to use everyday items as weapons and be prepared to use them, if necessary.

When outside, one might consider how to cross a street with no crosswalk, or the usage of caution when going on to trains, automobiles and so on.

For examle, when riding on a train, ride on the middle car instead of the front or the last one. In case of a sudden stop or an accident, less damage is to be experienced in the middle. I often ride the bullet train to go to the Kansi area, but I have seen situations where the overhead luggage fell off due to a sudden stop and seriously injured passengers. With the vibration inside the train, luggage will fall eventually, but not directly below but in the direction of the train's travel. I have no knowledge of physics, but this phenomenon has something to do with gravity and the train's speed.

The point being, it is important to be aware of those around you. Especially nowadays in society when signs and people can come falling off from any building, preparation of one's mind is necessary at all times. Not to the extent of paranoia; but as a course of habit.

I myself had such an incident near the Nihon-hashi in Tokyo. It was quite windy and a sign from a nearby building undergoing some construction came flying towards me. I was able to avoid it at the last second, but the person who was walking beside me suffered an injury. This kind of occurrence is not about odds as in a lottery, but rather, misfortune.

Do not walk around when it is not necessary to do so, shut all doors and windows in a storm and so on. Sharp or cornered objects that can suddenly become harmful instruments should not be placed within easy reach. In the past, people would take precautions in order to avoid embarrassing or even threatening situations later. These kinds of precautions should still be taken in the present as well. Especially those of parents - parents' actions greatly influence their children. Hence, we must all be careful of our actions.

眼，心，力，技は一体

The Eyes, Heart, Strength and Technique are One

Eyes speak just as loud as the mouth does. Angry eyes, happy eyes, cute eyes, embarrassed eyes, doubtful eyes, scared eyes, confused eyes, crazy eyes, sleepy eyes and so on all express some sort of state which one finds himself in.

These are all the result of the heart's actions shown through the eyes and made visible. The eyes are indeed the windows to the soul. Hence, looking at the eyes, one can see the soul. However, one can not look inside the soul through the eyes every time. If one has weak eyesight, or is blind, then one can not see the other's eyes and consequently not his soul either. Those with an evil soul would have dark eyes and his soul can not be determined. This is the kind of eye that is desirable in martial arts. Although one's punches and kicks may land and may make him seem like an expert, where one places his eyes is distracted by each movement, for example, in a low kick, one would tend to look down. In this case, no matter how expert he seems, he is simply just using the kata. That is because how one holds his heart naturally appears through the eye. If kata, the expression of the heart, and the heart itself are separated from each other, kata is meaningless.

In watching a marionette, if the person who is controlling the doll is genuine, then, his genuineness will show through in the movements of the marionette itself.

A kata that does not accompany a heart that possesses kata is dead. A "dead" kata has no meaning. The same can be said for an artist who paints with no soul in his picture. In every movement of a kata, there is a meaning or an objective. If one's movements do not incorporate these meanings or objectives, then no matter how long one practices, it is pointless.

If the kata is not "alive," then, obviously, it is "dead." Unless the kata is alive, it can not be utilized. And it is difficult to use a kata which is "lively." One must practice beginning with his heart, or he will never improve. Practice and training often begin in groups with a "call." Any movements are so, but it is in constant repetition to the calls of the instructor. Sometimes, it seems as if the instructor is just yelling to his students, while the students just perform a controlled dance of some sort.

All movements in martial arts exist with an opponent in mind. Even when being performed alone, one must envision his opponent constantly. In group training, one must consider his opponent as well; not just throwing punches ahead of him at air. Punches should be thrown in all directions and kicks, blocks and other defenses should never be ignored. These actions, in sequence, form kata and was formed so that one could practice by himself.

What is important is that no matter which direction one faces, after completing one movement, he should be able to react in any direction afterwards. That is, when punching forward, how about behind? If one is not careful, he will collapse his posture for a punch. In every instant, one should be able to react in any direction around himself. This kind of posture is the expression of this kind of mind-set. Thus, the eyes may be seeing forward, but the heart must be looking in all directions. If the heart only "sees," in one direction, then one's posture favours that direction as well and disallows sudden reaction to any other direction. This not only applies to the heart, but to strength as well.

Of course, strength works as the heart does, to the relationship between the heart and strength is similar to that of heart and posture; similarly, strength and posture can not be separated either. Strength must be maximized when one makes contact with his opponent, but must return to a "normal" level immediately, in order to react to the next situation, simultaneously. Therefore, strength is not used until the very moment contact is to be made. Strength is not necessary before or after the moment of contact. Strength must be distributed evenly throughout the body and the center of that distribution can not be altered under any circumstances.

If the centre of distribution remains at the center of one's body, there is no fear of collapsing one's stance after contact is made, nor is there any fear of not being able to shift that stance after contact is made with the opponent. When too much strength is placed in the arms when punching, or too much strength is placed in the legs when kicking, it becomes difficult to alter the stance of the body because the centre of distribution of strength is altered. The same applies to the heart - if the heart is too preoccupied in one direction, the centre is lost and as a result, the heart can not distribute itself evenly in all directions. However, the heart can not remain in the centre as well. The heart can not leave the centre of its distribution, yet it must be distributed. The heart requires to not be distributed, but desires to do so.

Like messenger birds; they are free to fly to deliver their messages, but they always return to their home. It is not visible, but this occurs because there is a connection between the birds, their hearts and their body.

Karate is no different from this, as there must be a connection between strength and heart in order for the heart and body to become one. Technique is an expression of the heart. Technique can not separate from the heart and vice versa. The eye, also an expression of the heart, is the same - it can not be separated from the heart. If the eye concentrates on one fixed location, the heart follows, leaving its center. Similarly, if the heart stops in one place, then the eyes can not see.

In training for karate, when one stares at the opponent's eye, fist, legs, soon, his heart becomes fixed at this location. The same can be said for the heart - the eye then becomes fixed at the location. The eyes and the body's technique all operate from the command of the heart, hence, the preparedness of the heart is most important. Thus, an "unfixed" heart is desirable. The apex of karate training lies in the training of the heart. Eyes are important to human beings, but sometimes they can interfere as well.

There is a story of a blind teacher who's teachings were asked to be stopped by his students because the storm had shut the lights down. Instead, the teacher was said to have laughed at his students because they can see. Hence, eyes that can see everyday things may be inconvenient at times. The excitement one feels when seeing someone attractive, or the fear that one feels when he sees something terrifying all occur because he is able to see things. These things enter through the "windows" which are the eyes and affix themselves at the heart. What matters is not the eyes, but the heart, which is the master of the eyes. Training of the martial arts serves to control the heart and not react so suddenly. One can remain calm under any situation if his heart is prepared properly. It is important to constantly keep the heart in such a state.

"Sen-shin" is one objective of martial arts training. However, will there ever be such a heart that will always remain calm through long years of training? To ask a question as such means that my heart is not calm. But when, for example, faced with death, is there an individual who can say that his heart is calm?

> *There is a story as follows:*
> *A Buddhist priest, trained for numerous years to withstand any kind of pain and anguish asked his doctor to tell him the nature of his illness - so, the doctor told the priest it was cancer - the formerly confident Buddhist priest who was supposedly able to withstand any pain or anguish began to cry and eventually died in tears.*

I believe this story to be true. Human beings all fear death the most. That death is inevitable - no one can escape from it. It would be admirable if one sought death, welcomed it and died. Martial arts training - any training for that matter - is only a method of training for the heart. However, with only this kind of training, it seems hopeless. In order to remain calm and unmoved in the face of death, one must not have any attachments to the world when he dies. In order to reduce the amount of attachments one has to the world, it is best to not have any regrets or sorrow for past actions but to have satisfaction and joy in life. I think everyday life and actions influence the training of everyone's heart.

Whatever objective that each individual seeks to achieve in life - with no regrets - until the moment of death, and the achievement of that objective is the only feasible answer, I think. The method is easy - it is the realization of this that seems to be so difficult. As a matter of fact, human beings nowadays have a weakness due to the relative easiness of their lives. It would be desirable to see that all human beings co-operate to achieve a harmonious state by living a lively, joyful, satisfying and fulfilling existence. If a calm, unmoving heart is obtained or achieved, the eye that expresses this kind of heart would truly be beautiful. Martial arts training, which is the training of one's heart, does not occur only within a dojo. It is often said that: "One is constantly in training to better himself." How true this is.

体力, 気力, 技力

Physical Strength, Mental Strength, Technical Strength

No matter which martial art, it is desirable that these three elements excel for every individual. Training does help, but talent, (what one is born with) also separates the good from the worse.

Of the three, if any one of them excels the opponent's, then, one has that much advantage over him. If physical and mental strength are identical, then technical strength becomes the deciding factor. And so on and so forth.

If one strength is below that of the opponent's level, if another strength is particularly excellent, then that strength can cover for the weaker strength. Even if one is physically weak, his technical superiority may put him at an advantage. However, even if physical and technical strengths excel, if the mental strength is not sufficient, the former two can not be well utilized.

If any of the three is too weak, then it will serve as the downfall of that individual. There can be situations where a small person beats a bigger, stronger, but mentally weaker person. Also, I have seen an individual's technical strength excel in training, but weaken considerably in a contest. This is because his mental strength is weak.

One can have mental and technical strength, but have little physical strength and lose. Sometimes, none of these even matters. In my youth, in the 7th year of the Taisho era, there was a contest between a foreigner, who was a wrestler and a Japanese judo expert. There were not too many individuals who belonged to the Kodokan at this time. The wrestler was quite skilled and handily defeated numerous others, but this judo expert was able to place the wrestler in an arm lock and lay him on his back. The audience was cheering for the judo expert, but something happened. The wrestler just got up, raised his left arm and shook the judo expert off. It was no contest. And I have heard many other similar stories.

If there is too much difference between the physical strengths of the opponents, it would be similar to me twisting an infant's arm. Especially nowadays, when non-Japanese individuals train in the martial arts, it is important for individuals to train hard in technique, physical strength and especially, mental strength. Also, one must also consider the differences in weight of the participants when a Japanese and non-Japanese engage in contest.

構えと受け

Posture and Uke (Posture for Defending)

There are many varieties of posture. There is no, one, fixed stance. In essence, a stance must be able to respond to any changes that the opponent makes, defend, or simply take the blow that the opponent strikes with.

However, in Japanese martial art, there is no defense whose prime objective is to simply defend. The prerequisite of defense is offence. Postures, similarly, are taken with offence as a prerequisite. There is no need to defend or even take a posture if attacking the opponent is not an objective. Posture is for offence and defense; defense is defense because one is not on the offensive.

Hence, attacking after defending results in a draw of attack, or one falls behind in the offensive. It must always be defend / attack, or attack / defend. Since offence is the prerequisite of both posture and defense, these must both be able to produce an attack immediately, as well as being able to respond to any attacks in return. If this fact can not be seen in one's kata, then that kata is useless. If too much strength is placed in a posture, or if one's wrist is bent after punching, or if one looks down as he is kicking, these actions only serve to make that action meaningless. In essence, it becomes a "dead" kata.

To use a "live" kata is so difficult, that it may take ten or twenty years, even a lifetime of experiences to even begin using the kata properly. In kendo, one must constantly be prepared to withdraw his sword, even though the sword may not be drawn - this is similar to the posture in karate. If posture is not "alive," it serves no purpose. This can be found in any writing or book of any martial art.

待ち手と懸け手

Machite and Kakete

In a contest, there is both machite and kakete. Machite is the method with which one responds when the opponent strikes first; kakete is the opposite.

There are two kinds of machite. Kakete only has one. Win or loss is decided by these three.

The first of the machite, "gosen-no-te," defends and simultaneously attacks - hence, it is defend / attack. The second of the machite, "sensen-no-sente," strikes the enemy as he is about to make his first strike while defending that strike. Hence, one strikes before the opponent strikes. Hence, it is defend / attack as well. When defense and attack are separate, one is often pushed into defense only. It must be remembered that offense is also the best defense.

"Sente," the kakete, attacks first by catching the opponent off-guard, or forcing the opponent into such a state. Also, the opponent is not dumb - he will respond with one of the above three; thus, one must be careful to not fall victim to it himself. Therefore, these actions go back and forth; in addition, remember to maintain a good mindset and a good pocket of space between you and the opponent.

武の業は　宇宙の如く　無限にて
業に極致は　なきものと知れ
博紀

'Martial art technique is like the cosmos, it is infinite.
Know that there are no such things as limits.'
- Hironori Otsuka

実技篇

TECHNIQUE

指掌の部分名称

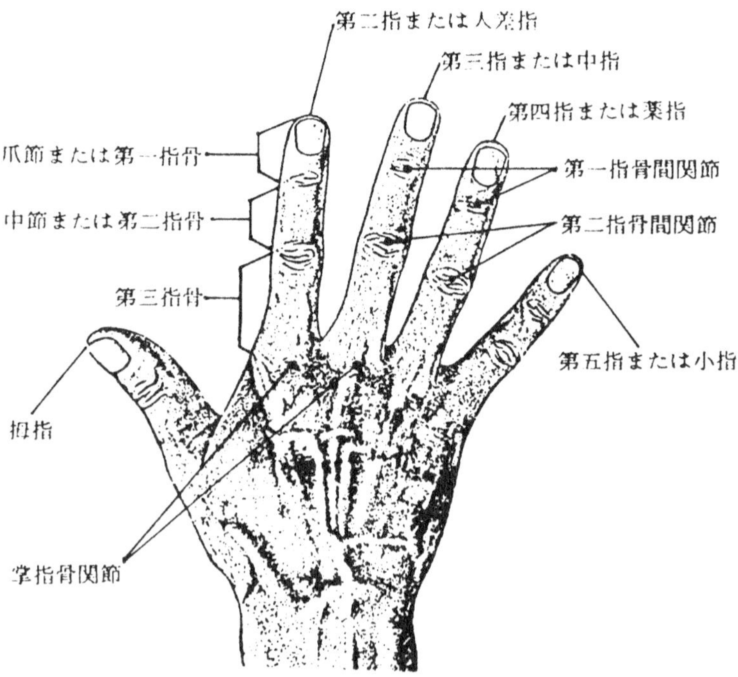
第二指または人差指
第三指または中指
第四指または薬指
爪節または第一指骨
第一指骨間関節
中節または第二指骨
第二指骨間関節
第三指骨
第五指または小指
拇指
掌指骨関節

基本の動作

FUNDAMENTALS OF MOVEMENT

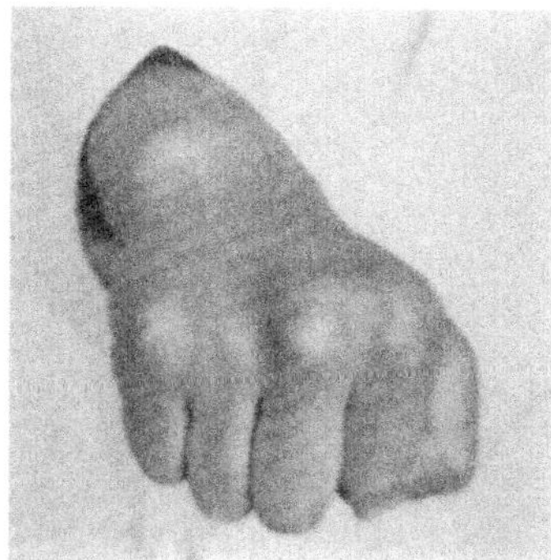

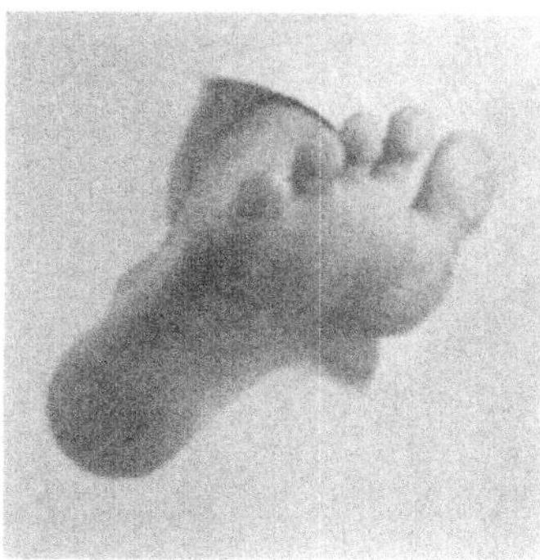

PARTS OF THE HAND AND FINGERS

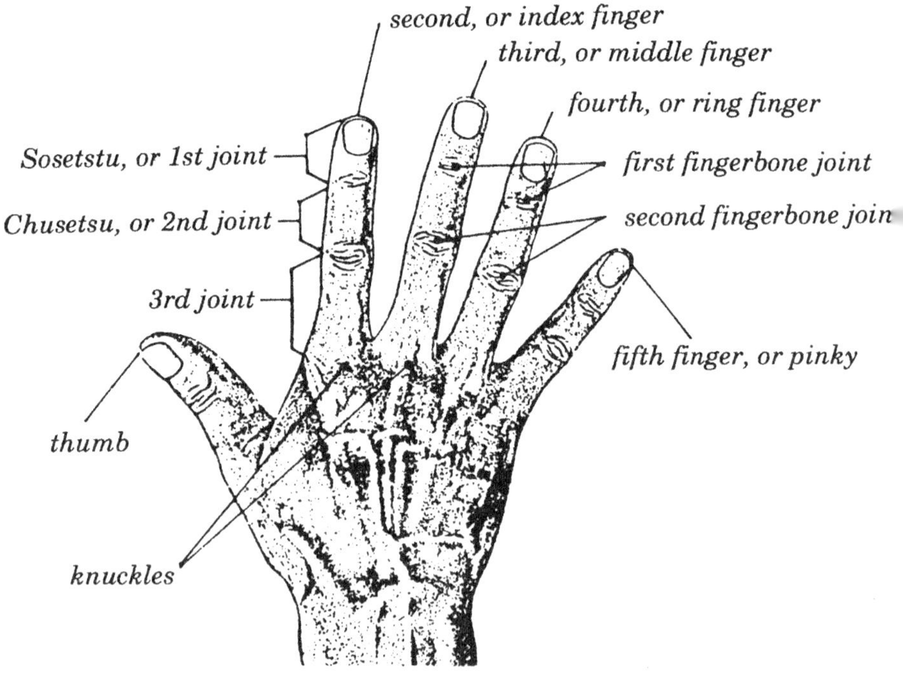

拳の種類

CLASSIFICATION OF FIST STYLES

Fist 1 is the most commonly used form and is seen quite often, however, punching an opponent's face, requires caution because one can be hurt from hitting the opponent's teeth. For hitting the face, use Shuto or Nekote instead of the fist, as shown.

Strike in line with the middle of the arm. Essentially, pull the fist behind one's shoulder and thrust at the level of one's chest's middle. Thrust straight forward. The knuckle of the middle finger should be horizontal. Following punches are to be like the first punch. I leave any changes to this in accordance to the situation.

FIST 1

Hold all fingers except the thumb firmly as if to grip something, while bending the thumb at almost 90° and covering almost two thirds of the index finger and one will see that power begins to concentrate upon the center of the fist. One punches with the knuckle of the middle finger, but the second joint of the index finger may make contact as well; hence, it is important to grip firmly.

FIST 1

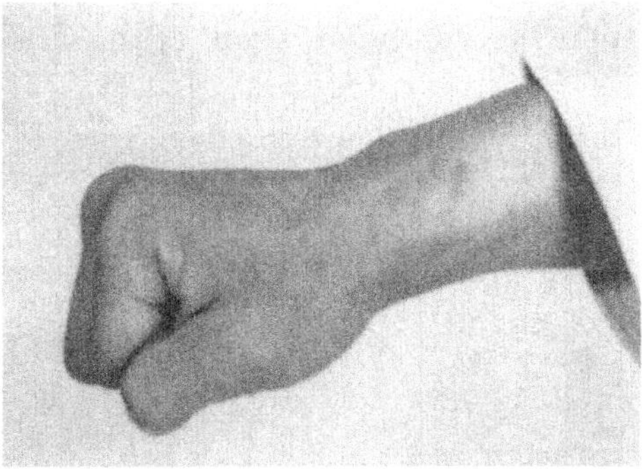

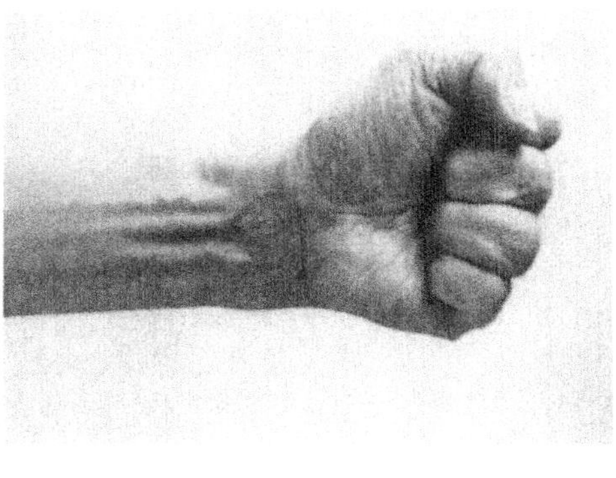

FIST 2
The middle finger first. Slightly release the middle finger, yet grip firmly as in Fist 1. Grip the first and second joints of the middle finger firmly with the index and ring fingers and strike with the second joint area of the middle finger.

Excellent when used against the head, chest or anywhere with bone immediately beneath the skin; or shoulders, thighs and anywhere with muscles. Also good for striking the eyes.

FIST 3
Hold the second finger-bone joint of the index finger with the thumb, so the thumb does not protrude towards the palm of the hand. Grip the hand to only make contact with the index, middle and ring-fingers.

Excellent for striking the head, forehead, face, or body of the opponent. Also used in hitting the opponent's arm in a punch, or a leg that is about to kick. Depending on the situation, one may incorporate a "snap" in the wrist.

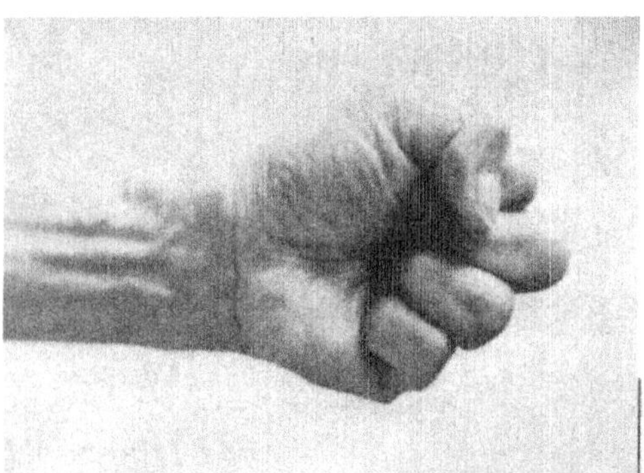

FIST 2

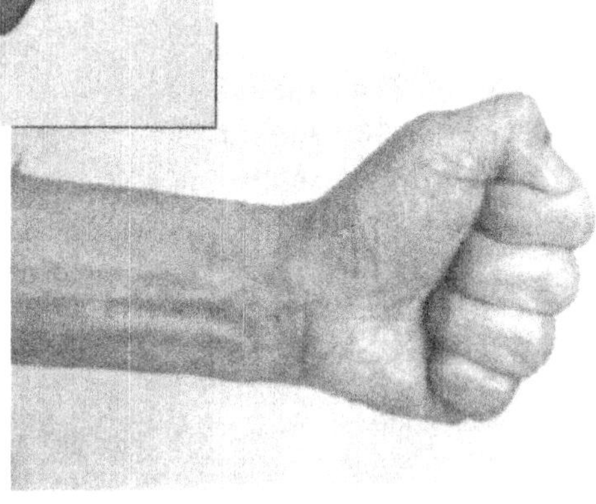

FIST 3

FIST 4

Let the index finger loose slightly, push it against the middle finger and hold the thumb over the middle finger. Strike with the area that is on the outer side of the index finger. Be careful not to injure the thumb when striking.

FIST 4

FIST 4

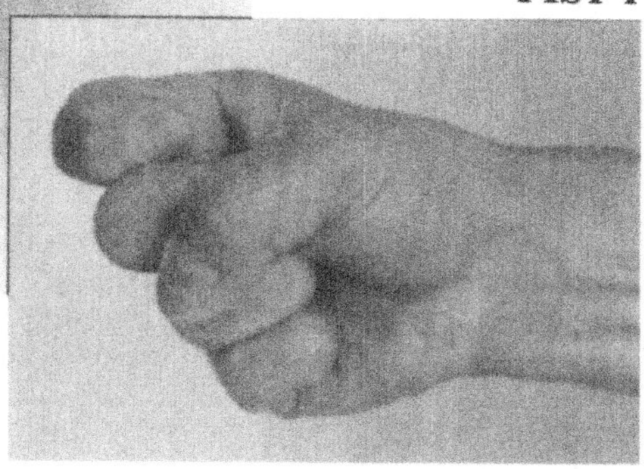

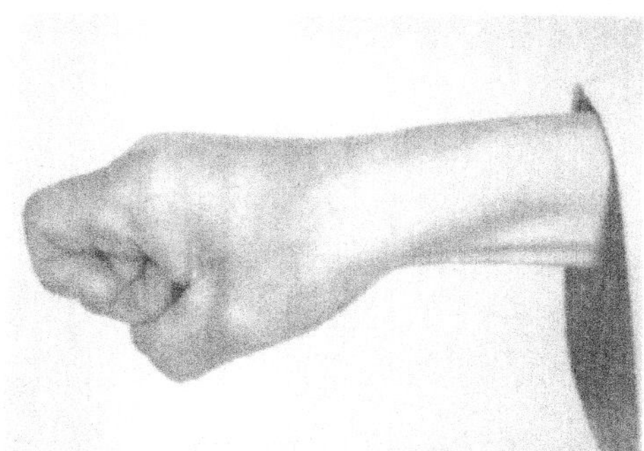

FIST 4

FIST 5

Let the thumb from Fist 4 loose a little, in order to create a small "ring" with the thumb and index finger; this allows the chin to fit inside the "ring" and lessens any injury to the fist.

This is used to strike the opponent's chin from below. Use a snap of the wrist when striking.

FIST 6

This is called "Koosaa" in Okinawa. Let the index finger loose slightly and adhere it to the middle finger and place the first joint of the thumb along the outer side of the index finger.

Can be used to strike the face, chest, or other areas where bone occurs.

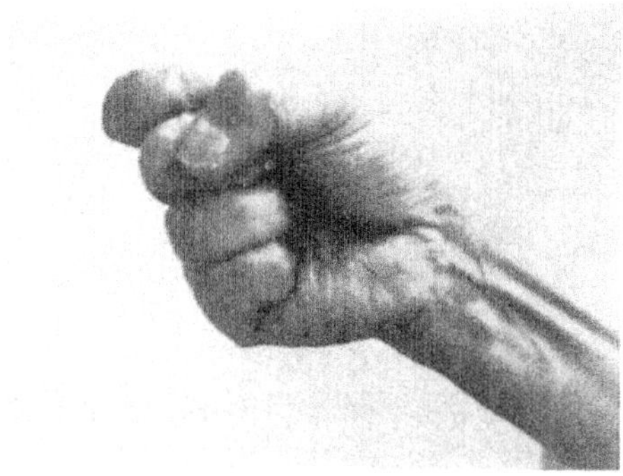

FIST 5

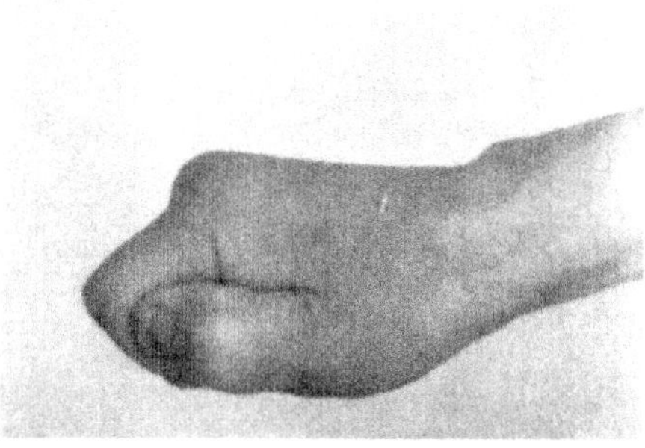

FIST 6

手刀の種類

CLASSIFICATION OF SHUTO STYLES

SHUTO 1

Called "shuto," also known as "tegatan." All fingers except the thumb are extended and held together, while being bent slightly inwards. Strike with the outer side of the small finger, or use in defense. This can be used to strike downwards on the head, forehead, face, throat, shoulder, body, upper thigh and so on, as well as striking sideways. It can also be used to defend from an opponent's punch or kick.

SHUTO 2

Slightly bend the four fingers inwards and place the thumb in the palm as if to push against the four fingers, while making sure that the thumb does not exceed the edge of the palm. This shuto is used to stab with the fingertips and thus the above form is taken to not injure the thumb. Some individuals do spread the fingers apart to strike at both eyes of the opponent. This is dangerous since the opponent can defend with a shuto himself and grab one's fingers and force them apart. Mostly used to stab at the eyes and abdomen.

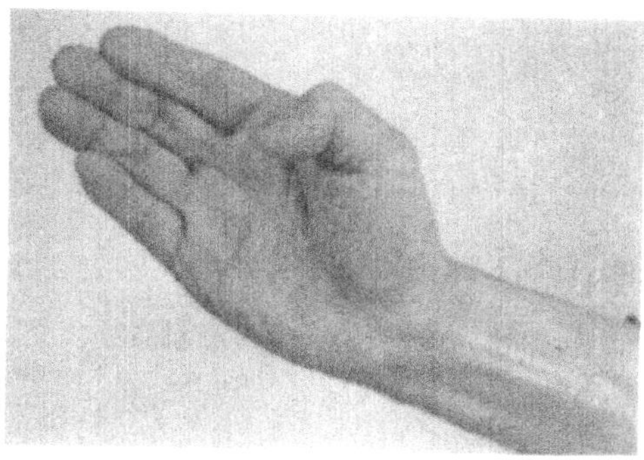

SHUTO 1

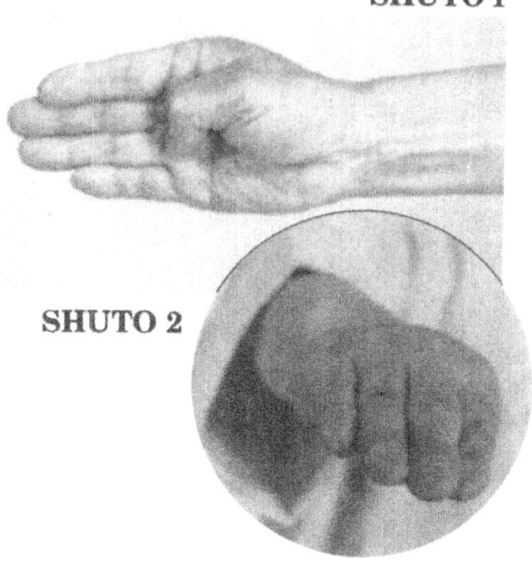

SHUTO 2

SHUTO 3
It is called "nekote" in some forms of jui jitsu. All five fingers are bent at the finger-bone joints and the thumb is bent slightly backward as to not be in front of the palm.

Using the lower area of the palm, used in attack and defense. Most often used to strike the nose or striking the opponent's chin upwards. This also becomes a shuto when the side is used.

SHUTO 3

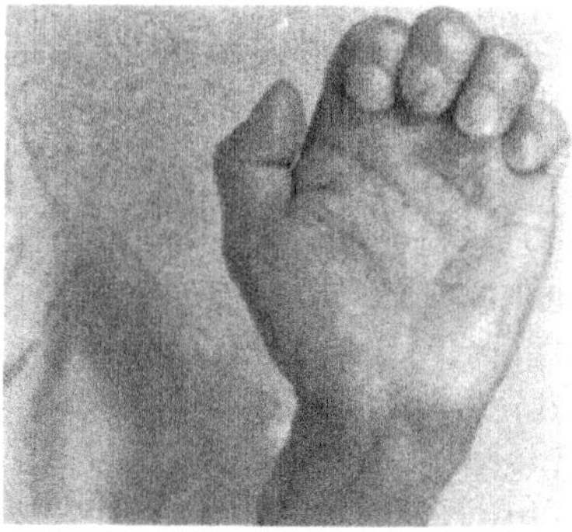

SHUTO 2

SHUTO 3

SHUTO 4

This is known as "kumate" in some forms of jui jitsu. Open all five fingers slightly and bend the fingers at the first and second joints slightly, as if to form a rake with the hand.

Used to scratch the opponent's eyes (especially in a kumite).

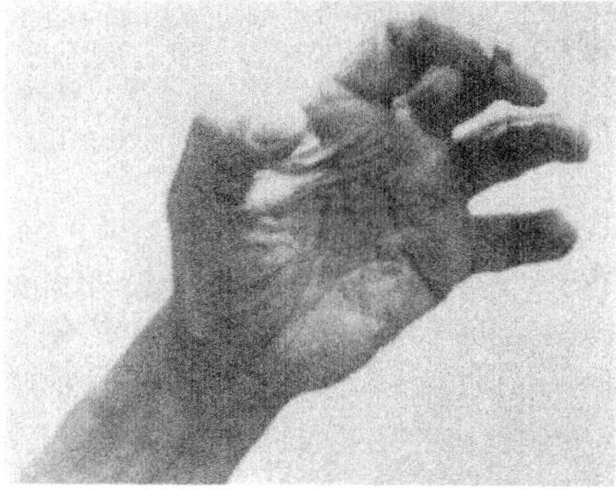

SHUTO 4

SHUTO 5

Extend all fingers except the thumb and place some space between each finger, while placing the thumb inside the palm.

Used to often fake a strike or punch. Can be used to strike at the face, eyes, or nose of the opponent.

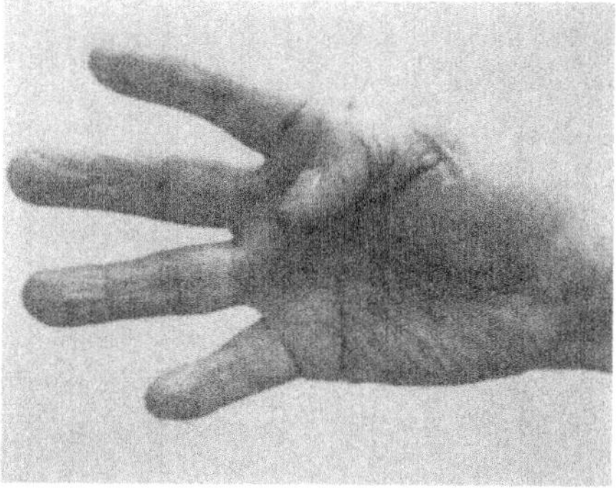

SHUTO 5

SHUTO 6

Place all fingers except the thumb together and bend slightly along with the thumb in order to create a semi-circle with the hand.

When in close contact with the opponent, this can be used to strike or grab at the opponent's throat.

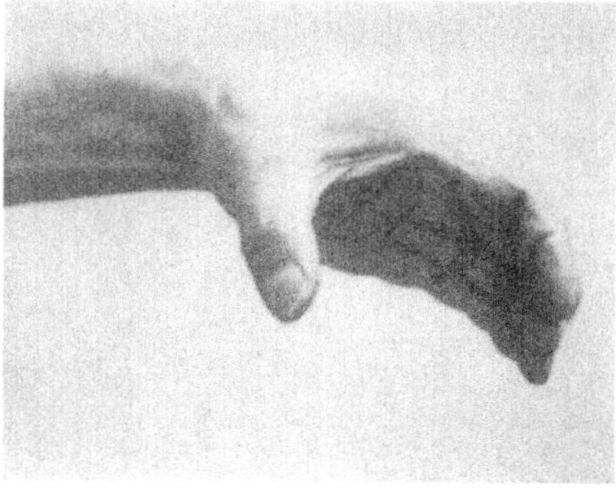

SHUTO 6

SHUTO 7

Place the fingertips of the thumb, index, middle and ring fingers together, while adhering the small finger to the ring finger.

With the tips of these four fingers, strike as if a bird would strike its prey. When grappling with an opponent, this is used to surprise the opponent - thus, it does not matter where one strikes. For example, strike at the stomach, head, hands or eyes.

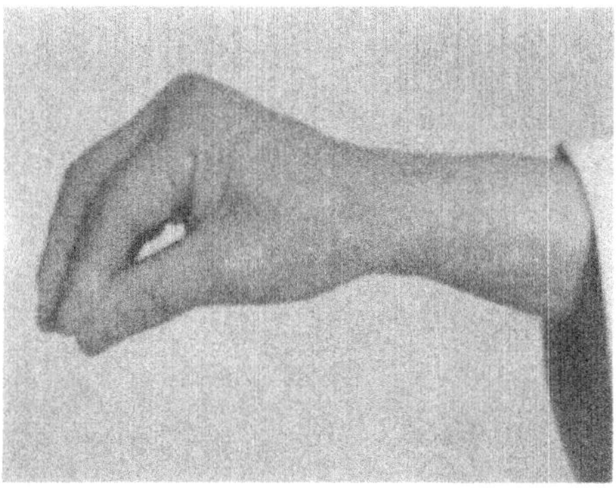

SHUTO 7

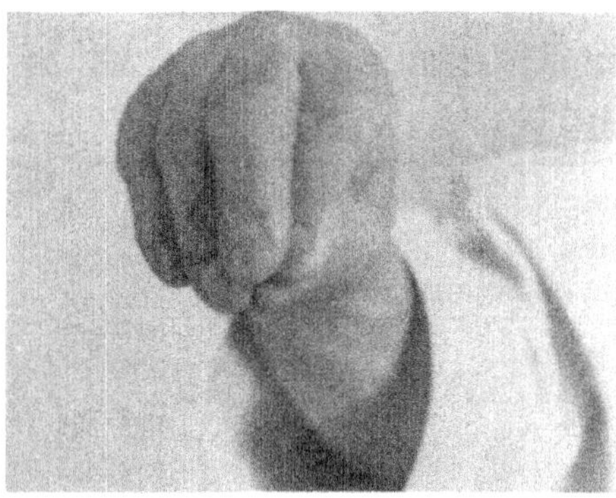

SHUTO 7

蹴りの種類

CLASSIFICATION OF KICKING STYLES

(1) ASHI-URA

Using the soles of the feet, one can use this in a front kick, a side kick and so on, to strike virtually anywhere on the opponent, including the head, forehead, side, thighs, lower abdomen and so on. Make sure to bend the toes upwards.

Sometimes, a kick is done by curling the toes inwards, but without much practice, one risks spraining his foot.

(1) ASHI-URA

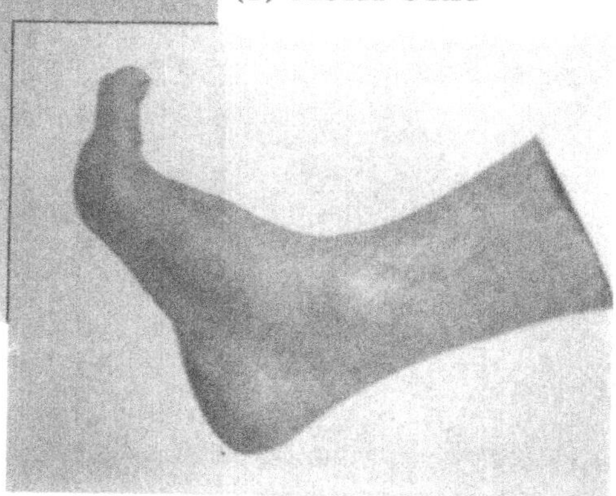

(2) SOKU-TO
Using the outerside of the foot, this can be used to kick forward and in, or to kick up with. Kick forward at the stomach and knees and kick down at the elbows and so on.

(3) SOLE
Using a backwards roundhouse kick, the sole can be used to kick at the knee and connecting joints, or lower stomach and so on. (not pictured)

(4) INSTEP
This can be used to kick at the opponent's leg, stomach, forehead and head.

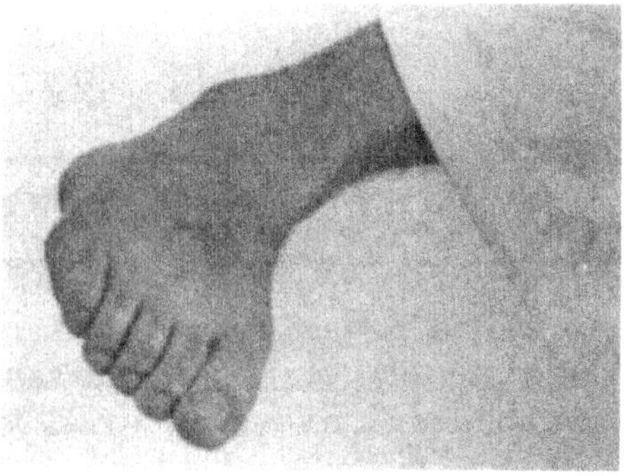

(2) SOKU-TO

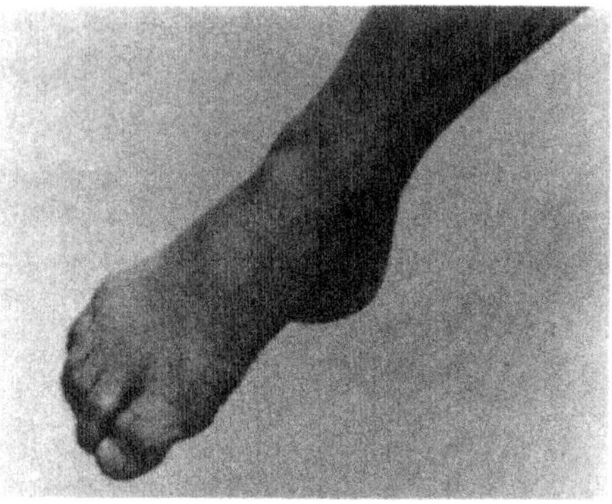

(4) INSTEP

(2) SOKU-TO

立ち方の種類

CLASSIFICATION OF STANCE STYLES

(1) KIRITSU

Heels are placed together, with the toes slightly apart from each other; eyes forward and arms at the sides. Very first stance of every movement.

(2) JUN-TSUKI-DACHI

This refers to the situation when the fist of the same side of the kicked leg is about to be used. Hold the upper body straight, placing one's weight equally on both legs while slightly bending the knee of the forward foot making sure that the knee does not exceed the toe, while performing this movement. When the knee of the hind leg is straightened, it tends to throw the balance off; hence, do not tighten nor bend the knee of the hind leg, but just maintain the knee to maintain one's balance.

(3) GYAKU-TSUKI-DACHI

The opposite; when the fist from the opposite side of the foot being stepped out is about to be used. In order to maintain balance, here, the front leg is placed slightly outwards and the toes of the hind leg are pointed slightly inwards and both knees are very slightly bent. One's own weight should still be held at the centre of one's body.

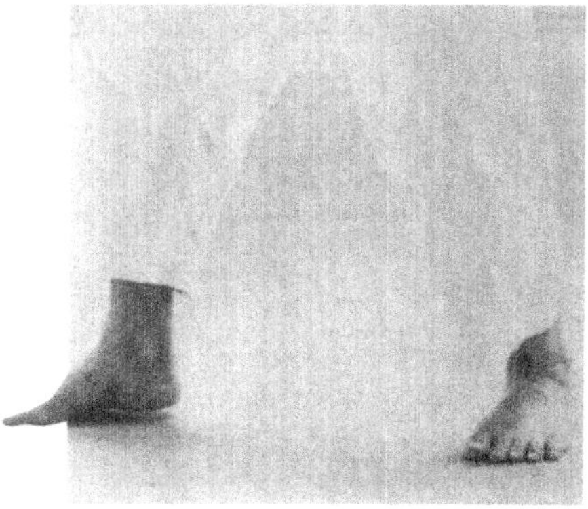

(2) JUN-TSUKI-DACHI

(3) GYAKU-TSUKI-DACHI

(4) THRUSTING STANCE FOR JUN-TSUKI

By straightening the hind knee and leaning forward with the body (the front knee bends forward), punch. The hind toes face to the side, while the front toes face forward to increase force. If one is to strike with the right fist, step forward with the right foot and so on. Be careful not to align the heel of the front foot with the heel of the hind food, as this serves to weaken the punch. The toes of both feet should be perpendicular to each other, but not crossing the heels. Lean forward with the weight of the body, but not so much to lift the hind leg off the floor. Be prepared to alter these stances at any time, for whatever reason. I will elaborate later.

(4) THRUSTING STANCE FOR JUN-TSUKI

(5) THRUSTING STANCE OF GYAKU-TSUKI

Lean forward and punch using the whole body's weight. The body's balance tends to become lost here, so take a wide, low stance to offset this.

For this, place the front leg slightly forward and spread both feet wide to the left and right. Because one twists the waist when punching, use the hind leg as a pivot to imagine a circle and the forward foot must rest upon the upper edge of that circle. Point the toes of the front foot slightly inwards, while turning the heel of the hind foot slightly outward to keep the sole of the hind foot flat on the ground even if the body's weight shifts forward; simultaneously keeping the knees flexible and being careful to not lean too far forward.

For example, with the left foot forward and right foot behind, move the right foot forward, open slightly, twist the waist to the right and punch with the left fist (pull back the right fist with the twisting of the waist), then enter into the next stance, to be able to punch with the right fist. Do not force the foot to move, but move the foot in accordance with the twisting of the waist.

(4) THRUSTING STANCE OF JUN-TSUKI

It would make sense to start practicing this by punching at a low target, because a high target tends to lift the body up and the hind leg as well. In gyaku-tsuki, stand so that the knees are slightly inside the feet's location. Do not punch with the strength of the arm alone, as this creates the tendency to lift the body up and forward, weakening the punch and turning one's head to the side. Always punch using the waist and the whole body.

(5) THRUSTING STANCE OF GYAKU-TSUKI

(6) SHIMATA-TACHI

The same as in sumo's "shimata-tachi."

(7) HANMI-TACHI

When the right foot is forward, point the right toe forward and turn the body halfway to the left. The left toe is pointed slightly towards the inside. Leave about half a step of space between the feet and keep the knees flexible, but not bouncing. Make sure that both feet are not aligned with each other. This is similar to the stance in jun-tsuki.

(8) MAHANMI-TACHI

Stand as in shimata-tachi, but in the case where the right-hand side is used, point the right toe at the opponent as well as the head. The left toe and left side of the body does the same if the left-hand side is used.

(6) SHIMATA-TACHI

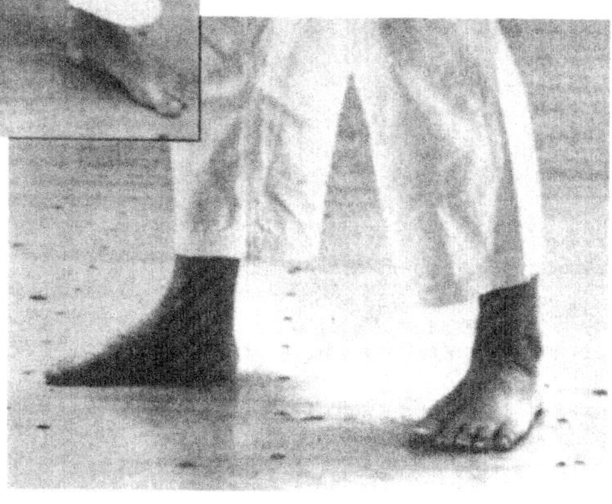

(7) HANMI-TACHI

(9) NEKOASHI-TACHI

First, straighten the upper body (in the case of left nekoashi-tachi), support the body's weight with the right foot and the left toe, while lifting the left heel slightly. The proper nekoashi stance has two thirds of the body's weight from the left toe to the right foot, and the remaining third of the body's weight on the right foot alone. Be careful not to shift the weight around from foot to foot. In a proper nekoashi stance, the upper body is kept straight, both knees are pointed in the direction of each foot, with the hind knee directly over the hind toe. Be sure to maintain the distribution of body weight at two thirds and one third.

For example, in the left nekoashi stance, the muscles in and around the right knee will tire easily - I will elaborate further, later.

HANMI-TACHI-NEKOASHI

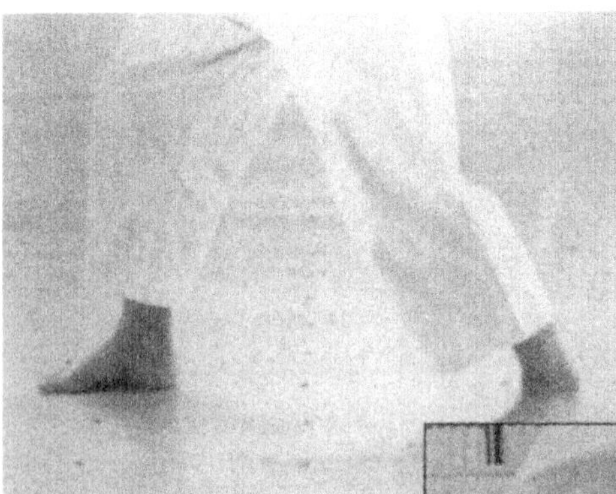

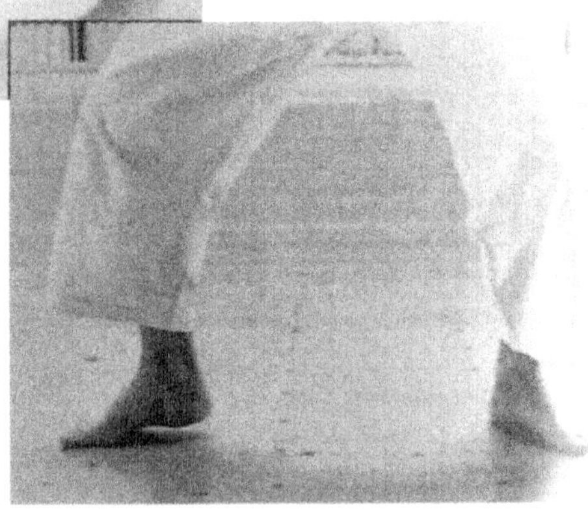

MAHANMI-TACHI-NEKOASHI

突きの種類

CLASSIFICATION OF PUNCHING STYLES

Punching and kicking are the most important in karate, they are its life. I will discuss their classifications and the importance of their method.

(1) SONOBA-TSUKI

Take the naihanchi stance. Lessen the space between the feet slightly, lower the waist slightly, place both elbows close to the chest, but behind the chest and grip both hands into fists. Both palms should be pointing upward. Punch forward with the left fist. The left fist should make contact with the middle of the opponent, preferably with the forearm being kept straight (at contact, the palm should be facing down). From this stance, alternately punch with the right and left fists. As one punches with the right, withdraw the left and return to the original stance. Repeat this alternately, constantly keeping the palm of the thrusted fist facing down.

Perform as follows.

(1) Both fists should be held as shown in Classification of Fist Styles - Fist 1.

(2) Do not grip too hard, but lightly.

(3) In the stance, keep the forearm horizontal and pull back sufficiently, but not so much as to place strain on the shoulders. This occurs when one tries to punch with the arms alone. The forearms are only slightly touching the side of the chest.

(4) Extend the thrusted arm completely. Do not bend at the elbows. Bending at the elbows is a sign of too much force or strength.

(5) Do not use strength before punching. Do not allow strength to remain after punching. It is only at the point of contact (this applies to defense as well) that strength is required. Strength before or after that moment of contact is a waste of strength and an interfering force for the next movement.

(6) Never use strength except at that point of contact. At that moment, use all the strength available to you. However, distribute your physical strength evenly.

(7) Don't forget to use your waist.

(8) Use your whole body when punching.

(9) Do not think of "punching," rather think of "pulling away." Think of "pulling and punching," not just "punching" alone. The rhythm of punching and pulling away must always be maintained. Don't think about pulling away, or else you will begin to punch with the arm alone. Use the body and waist as well. Although the whole body's strength is used, after the contact is made with the opponent, one's stance must return to such a state that allows him to react in any direction.

(10) When punching, in practice the punch should travel horizontally. From the side of the chest, the punch should maintain that height as it is released. The point at which contact is made should be the proper point on one's fist. Be careful not to twist the wrist as contact is made. Maintain a "line" through the centre of the arm you are striking with. When performed correctly, the knuckle of the middle finger should make contact first. Also, remember to incorporate a snap of the wrist into a punch whenever feasible.

Three main points of a punch (same in defense).

(1) Speed.
(2) Use the whole body.
(3) Twist the waist as you punch.

Imagine a small car hitting something and a large tractor trailer filled with sand in its back hitting the same thing. The force with which contact is made depends on mass and velocity, as demonstrated in: fs = 1/2 mv2.

This applies in karate also. Instead of using just the arm, if one uses the whole body, mass *m* above will increase. Using the pelvis as a pivot and twisting the waist to pull back on the left arm incorporates the same force into the right arm. It is logical. Twisting the waist increases the speed of the left fist. Also, the fist itself is twisted as contact is made, so the force of impact increases. Similar to the logic behind bullets, I suppose.

In the jun-tsuki which follows next, when the body moves forward with the punch, weight increases as well as velocity; hence, the force of impact becomes significant.

I do not excel in either physics nor human biology, so I am not able to explain this too well. I will not argue too much based upon science. Also, the velocity of the punch changes depending on the direction in which the punch is thrusted. When one attempts to punch with the arm alone, the elbow tends to lift and sends the punch upwards, lessening the velocity of the punch. And because the fist travels a lesser distance compared to when a twist of the waist is incorporated, velocity lessens.

In jun-tsuki, strength remains in the upper body, causing the hind heel to lift. To prevent this, one places force in his lower abdomen, which will prevent the heel from lifting, but cause the punch to lose force. In addition, in jun-tsuki, the body will tend to fluctuate up and down as a punch is being thrown. Thus, the punching arm can not be extended fully and the speed of the punch itself declines. A straight line from the fist to the target is the shortest distance. When punching with the arm only, the fist still travels a short distance, but it is weaker; it is like stabbing sideways with a spear instead of stabbing forward.

Extend the middle finger of the punching fist to see what I mean. If no strength is placed before a punch is thrusted, the punch will move more swiftly and have a great effect on the opponent. The fist will naturally travel the shortest distance possible. Punch as if your arm was a piston. Your extended middle finger will be as a spear, as you try the above. It is not all about "power" or "strength," but rather a "sharpness" in one's punch that matters the most. At rest, the fist and the body must be able to instantly react to anything from any direction. The same applies to one's heels - the heels must be prepared to shift the body in any direction without hesitation.

(2) JUN-TSUKI

"Jun-tsuki" is actually a word taken from jui-jitsu. It refers to the situation when the arm with which an opponent is punched is on the same side as the foot being placed forward and the reverse is called gyaku-tsuki.

When the right fist is used with the right leg being placed forward, it is called "migi-jun-tsuki," and conversely, if the left arm is to be used instead with the right leg, it would be called "hidari-gyaku-tsuki."

(2) JUN-TSUKI

To practice jun-tsuki, begin from the kiritsu stance and step forward with the left foot while punching with the left fist and placing the right fist at the right side of one's chest. Do not use just the arms and feet, but extend them using the whole body. Do not forget to use the waist here and pull back on the right elbow sufficiently to make the right forearm horizontal. Then punch hard with the left fist.

Every movement occurs with the whole body; never with the arms or feet alone. With arms alone, no speed results. One must not forget speed, the body and the twist of the waist. Things such as the length of a step, location of the waist and so on differ with every individual, so these become variables. The space between the feet can not be too narrow nor too wide. Both knees are to be flexible - firm, but not fixed. Make sure that knees do not point inwards when taking a step or producing a kick. The hind knee should be comfortable; not outstretched or bent too much.

The waist, too, can not be too high or too low. Both soles of the feet should be placed flat on the ground and place no strain on the ankles. Practice makes perfect. One stands with his whole body and not just his legs alone. In the second movement, the front foot should open slightly to the outside, or else it will be difficult to follow with the hind foot. But open the stance as the step is being taken.

The legs do not carry the body; the body carries itself. The legs which support the body must take an appropriate form for that support. The body moves as one's brain commands; both legs naturally follow the body. When the legs carry the body, the body moves up and down, slowing the speed of forward motion and hence lessening the impact of any punches being thrown. In noh plays and indigenous folk dancing, nobody "walks" with their feet. They walk with their whole body; the feet just smoothly follow. The same applies in karate.

Do not drag or pull them along, but lightly step with the feet. If one practices upstairs, those beneath you should not hear you practice. Again, it is not strength that matters, it is the "sharpness" with which a movement is executed. Also, in group training, some execute a punch before a call is made by the instructor. This habit makes it difficult to execute other movements in other directions. The stance one takes must be able to react in any direction, after its completion. If one punches forward from habit, the body tends to move forward, also and the hind heel lifts off the floor. To prevent this, some lower their waist too much, or thrust their lower stomachs; further complicating their error. At the end of every single movement, one must be prepared to react to anything in any direction.

(3) KICK, THEN PUNCH

A kick can be said to be one characteristic of karate. There are numerous kinds and sometimes, kicks are used in sequence. From the front kick to sokuto, from the front kick to roundhouse kick and so on, in a myriad of combinations and possibilities. Of course, the reverse of these can also occur. Kicks are not performed with the feet; but with the waist and the whole body. Any and all kicks are so. A front kick incorporates the waist and "kicks" with the whole body. A kick is never a simple extension of the knee joint. Like a fist, power is required at only one instant and speed is important. I will elaborate later, but as a punch, a kick must be performed just as quickly as it is withdrawn. Be flexible at the knees so one can react suddenly to anything from any direction and to maintain the body's stability.

When going from a front kick to a front punch, the kick turns into a step as one steps down with that foot. As one thinks about producing the punch, the kick gains momentum and falls as the kick is done. Hence, the fist is then ready to strike. Do not withdraw that foot, since this will serve to lessen the impact of the punch as it hits. Often, one is struck just as the kick turns into a step. This strike from the enemy is quite effective; use caution. One does not always have to follow a kick with a punch. After a kick is done, remember to be ready to react to anything from any direction. The time to switch from a kick to a punch is very short. But it is in this time where one must be in a stance to produce a punch. Be sure to remember: every single movement made must be "alive."

Sometimes, there will not be enough time to withdraw the arm of a punch, or a leg of a kick. Hence, immediately after execution, one must be in a position to perform the next appropriate and feasible action. All attacks increase their force of impact in accordance with how quickly they withdraw from their attack. I will explain this later on. When stabbing with a spear, it is said, "Stab at 30%, withdraw the spear at 70%." These are words to remember.

(4) GYAKU-TSUKI

When a gyaku-tsuki performed with a stance of the jun-tsuki, unnecessary strength is placed at the legs - hence, the stability against attacks from the sides is compromised. For example, if one stood on a thin beam, it would be quite easy to be shaken off from it. If one stood with his knees bent and weight spread out evenly over a wider beam, it would be difficult to shake him off.

When performing a gyaku-tsuki, the movement of the legs will be restricted if one punches with his arms alone - the hind ankle twists and lifts the outer foot. Thus, point the hind toe slightly inwards (not straight ahead), and punch with the twist of the waist as well. The front toe should be pointed slightly inward and ease the knees so the body may be lowered. There is less space between each foot, but more from left to right, when compared to the stance in jun-tsuki; thus, the body is slightly lowered. Imagine if something was to be held using the inner thighs (look at the naihanchi-stance).

One's weight rests on the knees and ankles. Also, the knees should not be directly over the toes on both feet, as the knees should be bent slightly inward.

(4) GYAKA-TSUKI

(4) GYAKU-TSUKI

(5) TOBI-KOMI-TSUKI

When striking with the right fist, one's stance becomes migi-hanmi and both fists are lightly placed at front (chu-dan stance, I will elaborate later). Both small fingers are pointed downward and both palms are turned inward, to face each other. The right fist will strike the opponent's face.

As one jumps forward with the right foot, he shall strike with the right fist. Simultaneously, the left fist shall be ready to defend. Often beginners fail to twist their waist - hence punch only with their arms. Face the right palm upwards (only slightly) and face the left palm downwards only slightly and as the right fist is about to make contact, place the left fist near the chest to defend. However, one must take the defensive stance as he is punching. Remember to pull away quickly after contact. As with the spear, "strike with 30% and pull away with 70%." The impact of a punch increases in relation to how

(5) TOBI-KOMI-TSUKI

quickly one withdraws that punch. (I will explain this later.)

However, fully extend the arm of the punch. When done, the fist being pulled back returns to the front of the chest. As at the start, the palms do not face up and both palms face inwards.

A word of warning when the arms are used instead of the whole body: the elbows rise, the fist does not travel straight forward and unnecessary strength will dwell in one's shoulder.

When returning to the hanmi-stance, do not pull the front leg back, but return the front leg using the whole body.

(6) OTHERS

There are others I do wish to illustrate. Nagashi-tsuki, Tobi-komi nagashi-tsuki and Tobi-komi gyaku-tsuki will all be elaborated later.

All must be performed using the strength of the whole body,

(5) TOBI-KOMI-TSUKI

quickly. For this, do not use any strength until the exact moment of contact. As physics dictate, using the whole body's weight, quick speed and the twist of the waist are most essential.

受けの種類

CLASSIFICATION OF DEFENDING STYLES

All defenses use the whole body's movement; not just the arms. Do not forget speed, the body and the waist. Furthermore, attack is a prerequisite of defense - hence, I will elaborate later.

(1) JODAN - DEFENSE 1

In the situation of a left defense. Using the left fist, strike upwards to the right from below at an opponent's attack, to punch it off, away from oneself.

If one uses the arms by themselves, the elbow rises and one would punch upwards, instead of striking upwards. If the opponent is physically stronger than you, one can not defend. Because one strikes upwards at the opponent's attack and forces it away from himself, he can defend against stronger opponents. Of course, in other situations, one would shift his body and pull the opponent's attack away from himself.

When defending from an attack, try to use an area close to the elbow rather than the forearm. Same thing applies when using the shuto to defend.

(1) JODAN - DEFENSE 1

(2) JODAN - DEFENSE 2

(2) JODAN - DEFENSE 2

Using the forearm, brush the opponent's attack to the outside. In this defense, if only the arm is used, one will not be able to absorb the impact - hence, never use the arm alone.

(3) CHUDAN - DEFENSE

When an opponent attacks lower than as in jodan defense, brush this attack off to the sides or the lower - diagonal sides. (not pictured)

(4) GEDAN-BARAI

(4) GEDAN-BARAI

In the left gedan-barai, twist the forearm outwards, place the fist (or a shuto) near the right upper chest lightly and stop an attack towards the left side of the body. The angle between the arm and the body should be about 40 per cent.

When using just the arms alone, one will see that his fist is pushed up towards his shoulder, hence, use caution.

Move with the whole body!

Every movement in karate is performed with the whole body; never with the four limbs. Thus, punch with the body, kick, defend, stand, pivot and walk, with the whole body. This can not be expressed on paper with my pen. The only way to gain this skill is through practice.

形 の 部

KATA

形について

ABOUT THE KATA

I first introduced Pin-an, however, there are so many with no name or origin. This is because they were once very secret and esoteric. Japanese martial arts were passed from mouth to mouth in the older days. This is because many people would misuse karate if it was too public.

In Okinawa, when weapons were first prohibited, karate was practiced in secrecy, by word of mouth. Hence, not many texts remain, if any. Pin-an starts from Shodan and goes up to Go-dan. In the latter years of the Meiji era, karate was made more public; thus, a karate expert named Ing Shu Ho was supposedly the one who originated Pin-an. Also, there was something similar in Okinawa called "Chan-an" but I do not know for sure. Of course there are some dissimilarities from that of those in Okinawa, however, what I am about to introduce are movements I have altered out of my own experience and knowledge.

Of the five kata in Pin-an, the Ni-dan kata is relatively simple, hence, most training begins with this kata. Some people pronounce "Pin-an" as "Hei-an" and call "Ni-dan" kata as "Sho-dan" and vice versa. This does not matter to me; change is inevitable. After Pin-an, one usually follows with Kushanku. "Kushanku" was the surname of a feudal man who lived about 220 years ago. This kata is very similar to Pin-an (so much, that maybe Pin-an derived from this kata) and imagines one's opponent to be located at the front, sides and behind one's self.

Next, Naihanchi is the kata that follows; however, this stance does not exist in Japanese martial arts. The most common ones nowadays incorporate the Shimata-dachi stance from sumo wrestling. Of course, in reality, this was a stance for karate and not sumo (look at the Naihanchi section). The only time one took a stepping motion was to move the body from side to side (look at movement #3, #8, #24). This probably came from Ing Shum who possessed a large frame and body. If one was to use the Shimata-dachi instead of the Naihanchi stance, then one ignores the most important objective of kata. If one wants to use the Shimata-dachi, then one should practice sumo, not karate.

Every technique has its own purpose. I personally favour Naihanchi. It is not interesting to the eye, but it is extremely difficult to use. Naihanchi increases in difficulty with more time spent practicing it, however, there is something "deep" about it. It is fundamental to any movement that requires reaction, I believe. Some people may call me foolish for my belief. I, however, prefer this over all else and hence I incorporate it into my movement. This has three katas, Shodan, Ni-dan and San-dan but the last two are almost useless. And from the Naihanchi stance, it is customary to follow with Sei-shan, which involves movement to all directions. Next, it seems most feasible to incorporate Chinto into the practice. Therefore, if Chinto can be grasped fully, that should be the "end." All other kata become the "stepping stones" to obtaining Chinti. I only incorporate nine kata into my movements. Some falsely believe that mastery and progress comes by knowing as many kata as possible. In the older days, one only knew about two or three at the most. Even to use one kata properly and efficiently is not an easy task. One must remember that it is quality over quantity when practicing any kata.

Each movement in a kata was made to be able to be practiced without an opponent - thus, they should all be considered as continuous, not singular motions separate from each other. Or else, one will encounter a problem as in movement #3 of Pin-an Nidan. But with movement #3 as an example, one must remember that the main objective of this is not lose the balance that the body possesses, in response to a kick from an enemy. Thus, when practicing, it is important to remember to imagine an opponent and remember the objective of that particular movement.

Kata is "alive" and not "dead." It must constantly be kept in mind that kata must be used in a "lively" manner. A dead kata is useless. After a period of time, one flows into one kata from another and begins to better understand the "feeling" that one movement incorporates into itself.

For example, in movement #8 of Pin-an San-dan, the shuto, loses its "feeling" because sometimes one flows into the next movement too quickly and one has the tendency to open the arms too excessively as if to "prepare" for the shuto. Thus, one must not think about what comes before or after, but on each and everyone of the movements that together make a kata. Of course, in some kata, a continuous combination may exist (for example movements #8 to #12 in Pin-an Go-dan) to which, what I just stated does not apply. Nevertheless, perform each movement properly. Imagine an opponent and practice until no stuttering occurs in the flow of kata movements.

I have mentioned warnings whenever they seem appropriate for each kata.

Simply, to master kata, one must practice and practice.

平安(ピンアン)初段

PIN-AN SHODAN

HOW TO STAND

Place heels together, spread toes apart comfortably, place both hands opened in front of you and look forward with the eyes.

Cleanse your mind and heart of any thoughts or emotions.

POSTURE FOR PREPARATION
With the left first, pull both heels apart and form fists with the hands. Grip lightly with both fists. About a foot's length between the heels. Remain natural - do not tense the arms, put strength in the stomach, or any other actions which deter the concentration.

All of Pin-an's five katas have the same posture of preparation.

The time to move from one posture to the next is a time at which the opponent may attack. If you are tense, you can not react immediately to any surprise attacks. Take care during these little "spaces" of time. Do not become careless in performing these movements. As stated earlier, use a "lively" movement pattern.

PIN-AN SHODAN

MOVEMENT #1

PIN-AN SHODAN

MOVEMENT #1

Point the left toe to the outside and using the Nekoashi stance, perform a jodan-defense with the left arm. Palm faces inward. Turn the head to the left.

The right forearm is placed in front of the head at the forehead's level, with the right palm facing forward.

To defend from any attacks originating from the left.

PIN-AN SHODAN

MOVEMENT #2

PIN-AN SHODAN

MOVEMENT #2
Keeping the head still, twist the upper body to the left while placing the left forearm to defend near the right cheek. The left palm faces the right cheek.

The right arm is stretched outward, pointing the small finger downwards to swing the arm down near the left shoulder.

The key points in this movement are the twist of the waist and the movements of the arms.

Make sure not to destroy the Nekoashi stance when twisting the upper body.

The lower body may lose its balance and one's posture may stretch upwards. If this occurs, there is too much strength in the shoulders. Although this posture may seem unnatural, practice it so that it no longer feels unnatural.

From movement #1, do not point the whole body to the left, but defend with the body as it was pointed. Of course, if there is actually an attack from the left, turn the whole body in that direction.

The twist of the waist serves to avoid the opponent's attack, while at the same time collecting strength for your attack. The waist's movement is very important here.

If the posture is incorrect, the left elbow rises and the forearm becomes diagonal. Human biology does not allow the right arm to stretch sufficiently and does not allow for a good defense. I do not believe that this defense can be ignored.

It is important to practice this until it becomes flawless. Practice so that one is able to attack in the same direction he is defending. This is obviously difficult, but this movement allows one to accustom himself. As stated before, kata is funademental, but it is also progressive.

As the left performs a Jodan-side defense and the right performs a Chudan-otoshi defense, both left and right perform defenses. But the left forearm must be able to become vertical for another defense and the right fist may strike at the side of the opponent's face. Hence, both the left and the right arms must be able to do as each needs to do, simultaneously.

PIN-AN SHODAN

MOVEMENT #3

PIN-AN SHODAN

MOVEMENT #3

Leave the head still and as the left foot is returned to its origin, twist the left arm and punch at the opponent's head (on the side with the small finger); withdraw the right fist and place near the chest.

The left fist travels at ear's height (head). Practice hitting the head with the left fist. When aiming high, there is a tendency to lift off the floor and raise the whole body. Practice so this does not happen - regardless of the target's location. Again, use the whole body to punch with. Practice, if this punch is uncomfortable. Movement #1, #2 and #3 are done continuously - but not hurriedly. Do not rush and carry these movements out smoothly.

PIN-AN SHODAN

MOVEMENT #4

PIN-AN SHODAN

MOVEMENT #4
From the posture in movement #3, do the opposite of movement #1 and on to the right hand side.

The right arm does not simply just rise; it performs a Jodan-defense.

As the right arm comes down, do not swing it in a big motion. If this happens, the left arm will move as well. This kind of motion is not useful; it is just action that is pointless. This kind of action puts unnecessary strength in the chest and serves to interfere with any following movements.

PIN-AN SHODAN

MOVEMENT #5

PIN-AN SHODAN

MOVEMENT #5
Movement #5 is the opposite of movement #2.

PIN-AN SHODAN

MOVEMENT #6

PIN-AN SHODAN

MOVEMENT #6
Movement #6 is the opposite of movement #3.

PIN-AN SHODAN

MOVEMENT #7 (1)

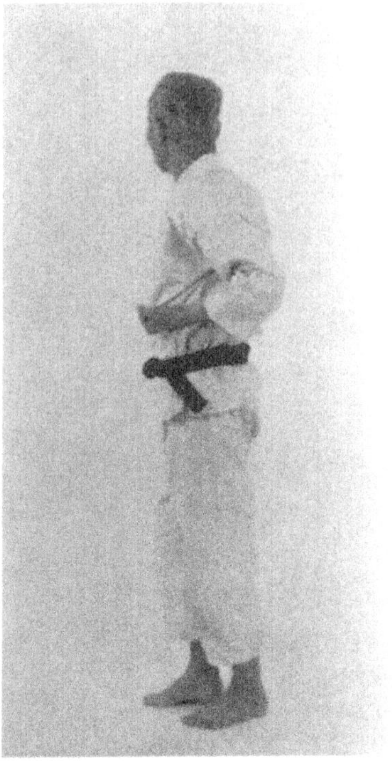

MOVEMENT #7 (2)

PIN-AN SHODAN

MOVEMENT #7

As the body moves to the right, do a Jodan-defense to the right with the right arm and perform a side kick to the right with the right foot simultaneously and turn the head to the right. The left fist remains.

The body moves to the right in defense from an enemy from behind, kick him as the body turn. Depending on the situation these movements can change one way or another. As the body turns, pull the right leg in before executing the kick. Thus, there are two steps here; before and after the right leg is pulled in. This is done simultaneously as the right hand is brought towards the body and as the body turns.

Defense, kick and turning the body must all be done simultaneously, so be sure to use "lively" kata and perform these movements swiftly with caution used on the location of the right arm.

As the body is turned, return the right arm gently to the right side of the body (do not tense these elbows), and raise them as a kick is performed; meanwhile, the left fist remains as is.

Twist the right arm inwards slightly and without bending the elbows extend the arm and lower behind to the right - the kick and defense shall occur together. If the right arm is lowered too quickly, the kick occurs too quickly as well and the kick and defense can not be come together. Practice this portion diligently.

PIN-AN SHODAN

MOVEMENT #8

PIN-AN SHODAN

MOVEMENT #8
The head is turned left as the right foot is returned to its place beside the left foot, placing the left foot forward in a nekoashi, while doing a Shuto Jodan defense to the left with the left arm. Bring the right hand in front of the chest.

This practice is to emphasize the Shuto Jodan defense (the change of direction is not too important), hence, use Mahanmi here.

For practicing the changing of directions, do this sufficiently so that the defense occurs simultaneously. (Pin-an San-dan, Movement #1.)

This is to defend from the opponent's Chu-dan strike, but it should be stated that it is difficult to perform the shuto - defense because the elbow has the tendency to rise. Do not bring the shuto down. This action does not help any. Kata expresses the objective of its action. Hence, the best way to improve is to practice in accordance to that objective.

Movement #7 and #8 occur continuously.

PIN-AN SHODAN

MOVEMENT #9
Take a step forward, place the right foot in a Nekoashi and perform a shuto jodan defense with the right hand, while placing the left hand, in a shuto, beside the chest. (not pictured)

PIN-AN SHODAN

MOVEMENT #10
Take one step forward and perform Movement #8.

In movement #8, #9 and #10 defend using the Mahanmi stance.

The shuto defense is difficult; use it with no excessive strength. Do the defense while shifting the body. Too much strength in the shoulder will result in a failed defense. Also, the body moves up and down sometimes as one steps forward. Again, too much strength in the shoulder will make the opponent strike your hand. Move the body smoothly and defend firmly. Practice this portion diligently. (not pictured)

PIN-AN SHODAN

MOVEMENT#11

PIN-AN SHODAN

MOVEMENT#11

Take a step with the right foot (stance for jun-tsuki), stab forward with a right shuto (small finger downwards) and the left fist placed by the chest.

Perform the shuto stab properly. Do not withdraw the shuto before it strikes; pull back on the left fist sufficiently.

Do not turn the body too much to the left, or the shuto risks missing its target.

PIN-AN SHODAN

MOVEMENT #12

PIN-AN SHODAN

MOVEMENT #12
Use the right leg as a pivot to turn around and bring the left foot in a Nekoashi 225° from where it stood, perform a left shuto jodan defense, while bringing the right shuto near the chest, against an enemy from the left diagonal rear. Possible to go towards the right and perform the same with the right foot and arm. This is done towards the left.

PIN-AN SHODAN

MOVEMENT #13
One step forward, right Nekoashi, right shuto jodan defense while placing the left shuto beside the chest.

PIN-AN SHODAN

MOVEMENT #14

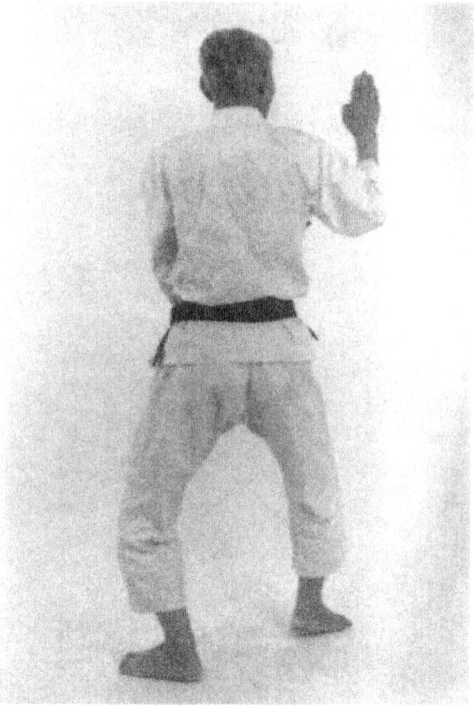

PIN-AN SHODAN

MOVEMENT #14
Turn the right Nekoashi 90° to the right and repeat the right shuto jodan defense. (pictured)

PIN-AN SHODAN

MOVEMENT #15
One step forward, left Nekoashi, do a left shuto jodan defense while placing the right shuto beside the chest. #8, #9, #10, #12, #13, #14 and #15 are to be performed with a Mahanmi stance.

PIN-AN SHODAN

MOVEMENT #16

PIN-AN SHODAN

MOVEMENT #16
Move the left foot 95° to the left, do a right jodan defense with the right fist, bring the left hand beside the chest and simultaneously twist the upper body to the left slightly. Twisting the upper body lessens the impact of the enemy's attack.

If defense occurs using the arm only, the elbow rises and the defense will not be done properly. Also, when turning, the body's weight will rest upon the right leg and the body may look awkward as it turns, so practice to correct this.

The right fist is used as the upper body twists and the left hand is vigorously withdrawn - these actions both add to the impact made by the right hand. Again, only use strength at the exact moment of contact.

MOVEMENT #17 (1)

MOVEMENT #17 (2)

PIN-AN SHODAN

MOVEMENT #17
Do a front kick with the right leg and a gyaku-tsuki with the left fist. The right fist is kept beside the chest.

Movements #16 and #17 are done continuously.

PIN-AN SHODAN

MOVEMENT #18

PIN-AN SHODAN

MOVEMENT #18
Do a left jodan defense. Turn the upper body to the right and do as in movement #16. The right fist remains as is. Lower the left arm diagonally left and defend as the upper body turns to the right.

If too much strength is in the arm, the elbow will rise and lock itself and the upper body will tend to lean too far forward.

In movement #16, a defense and a switch in direction occurs at the same time - hence, defend sufficiently, but not excessively.

PIN-AN SHODAN

MOVEMENT #20

PIN-AN SHODAN

MOVEMENT #19
Do a left front kick and a right gyaku-tsuki. Bring the left fist beside the chest. Movement #18 and #19 are done continuously. (not pictured)

PIN-AN SHODAN

MOVEMENT #20
Take a step forward with the right foot. Bring the left fist beside the chest. Switch from a gyaku-tsuki stance to a jun-tsuki stance.

The body moves up and down because the left knee extends to

"pull" the right leg forward. Do not defend with the hand after walking with the leg, but defend with the whole body after moving with the whole body.

When one advances with the right arm, brought diagonally downwards, (left) the defense naturally blends with the step being taken forward - hence, a good combination results. If the arm is pulled back too much, one advances, then defends. The reverse can also occur. Practice diligently. This kind of technique shows great effectiveness in actual use. If there is too much motion after any of the above actions, this creates a chance for the enemy to attack. Meaningful practice will bring a "lively" movement. At any time, be prepared to alter a stance to react to something.

In this situation, take a step forward and twist the waist to the left to defend and take the same posture as in jun-tsuki. The direction of the right arm and the twist of the waist will be in opposite directions.

Be careful to not turn in the same direction as the waist is turning - the left fist will hit the right elbow. (pictured)

PIN-AN SHODAN

MOVEMENT #21

Using the right leg as a pivot, turn 225° to your rear and do a left gedan defense, while placing the right fist beside the chest.

Turn the whole body sufficiently. Do not use the strength of the arm alone to defend. Also be careful that the space between the feet is not too narrow after pivoting. Remember to pivot with the whole body and to defend with the whole body.

Do not bend the upper body forward or look downwards. Maintain the upper body in a straight manner and look straight ahead. If a bad habit forms, it will show in a contest or combat. This is obviously dangerous, so never become careless, especially while defending. According to the situation, of course, the above may change slightly. Remember that "good" and "bad" are subjective.

But if possible, try not to alter the fundamentals. After all, a correct mastering of the basics allows for alteration.

This movement gives priority to the shifting of the body and gedan defense. Practice so that the body actually turns 225° since the whole body must turn. Never turn with the right foot alone. Practice to be able to turn to any direction.

PIN-AN SHODAN

MOVEMENT #22
Step forward with the right leg and do a right jodan defense, while bringing the left fist beside the chest.

PIN-AN SHODAN

MOVEMENT #23
Bring the right foot to the outside, turn 90° towards the right and do a right gedan defense. The left fist remains as is.

Be careful when shifting the body. Use the strength of the whole body as it turns to defend with the right arm. The left fist should not move from the chest area.

PIN-AN SHODAN

MOVEMENT #24
Step forward with the left, do a left jodan defense and bring the right fist back towards the chest.

PIN-AN SHODAN

MOVEMENT #25
Withdraw the left foot, lower both arms and return to the posture for preparation.

As at the beginning, do not tense up. Remain mentally aware and retain all cognitive senses. It is possible to encounter an attack at the very last second. Be prepared to react. If the heart is not relaxed, neither is the kata you are performing.

FINISH

Withdraw the left foot first, followed by the right foot and open both fists.

平安(ピンアン)二段

PIN-AN NIDAN

PIN-AN NIDAN

MOVEMENT #1

(Do the same as in Pin-an Shodan, movement #1. Look to the left and place the right fist at the chest.)

This movement is to defend against a Chudan attack from the opponent. Be careful not to place too much weight on the left foot, as balance will be lost. Lower the body. Do an uchi - otoshi defense. Defend with the body.

The left fist must be brought down by first raising the elbow and moving the forearm upwards. Use the right arm in conjunction with this, to increase the force of impact of the left fist.

Be cautious to not bring down the left fist using the arms alone as this will cause the elbow to rise as well as the waist.

Remember to use the motion of the right fist (pulling it into the chest area) to increase the force with which the left fist strikes.

PIN-AN NIDAN

MOVEMENT #2

PIN-AN NIDAN

MOVEMENT #2
Step left with the right leg, do a right jun-tsuki and withdraw the left fist to the chest.

MOVEMENT #3

PIN-AN NIDAN

MOVEMENT #3
Withdraw the right foot, turn around and do a right gedan defense.

This is not to only defend one's self from an enemy from behind, to interpret this action as such is a mistake. As stated earlier, kata is a combination of movements created to help train an individual. It would be wrong to assume that every movement is only for attacking or defending. The objective lies in the fundamentals. This movement incorporates both a shift of the body and a simultaneous defense, together, as one. Assume there is an enemy behind you. If one turns with his legs only, the body "remains" behind and he will not be able to defend properly.

PIN-AN NIDAN

MOVEMENT #4

PIN-AN NIDAN

MOVEMENT #4
Pull back the right foot a half step and strike downward with the right arm. Stop the arm at chest level. Extend the elbow to do an uchi-otoshi defense to the opponent's attack.

The foot is withdrawn to lure the enemy towards one's self. Hence, withdraw the foot with the whole body and not just the leg alone. Be sure not to bend the upper body forward or backward. Distribute your weight evenly between both legs. Extend both knees; do not bend them.

PIN-AN NIDAN

MOVEMENT #5

Take a step forward with the left foot, punch with the left fist and bring the right fist beside the chest. (not pictured)

PIN-AN NIDAN

MOVEMENT #6

Rotate the left foot 90° to the left and turn left while doing a left gedan defense. Do not move the right fist from its place.

PIN-AN NIDAN

MOVEMENT #7

Step forward with the right, do a right jodan defense and bring the left fist beside the chest.

PIN-AN NIDAN

MOVEMENT #8 & #9

Step forward and do a jodan defense alternately.

PIN-AN NIDAN

MOVEMENT #10

Using the right foot as a pivot, turn 225° and do a left gedan defense and bring the right fist to the chest.

PIN-AN NIDAN

MOVEMENT#11

Step forward with the right foot, do a right jun-tsuki and bring the left fist to the chest.

PIN-AN NIDAN

MOVEMENT #12
Move the right foot to the right and turn 90° doing a right gedan defense. The left fist remains as is.

PIN-AN NIDAN

MOVEMENT #13
Step forward with the left, doing a left jun-tsuki and bringing the right fist to the chest.

PIN-AN NIDAN

MOVEMENT #14
Move the left foot to the left and turn 45° doing a left gedan defense. The right fist remains as is.

PIN-AN NIDAN

MOVEMENT #15
Step forward with the right, doing a right jun-tsuki and bring the left fist to the chest.

PIN-AN NIDAN

MOVEMENT #16 & # 17
Alternately advance and do a jun-tsuki, then repeat.

PIN-AN NIDAN

MOVEMENT #18 (1)

PIN-AN NIDAN

MOVEMENT #18

Using the right foot as a pivot, turn left 225° and strike low with a left shuto while opening the body to the right and taking a Shimata-tachi (punch with the left). Bring the right shuto to the chest (palm facing up) and turn the head to the left.

While avoiding the enemy's attack, one attacks the enemy.

This is to practice both the shift of the body and a simultaneous attack.

Point the left shuto, left foot and face toward the direction of attack, turning the body and moving the right shuto beneath the left shuto (with the palms facing away from each other, left

PIN-AN NIDAN

MOVEMENT #18 (2)

palm facing up), and striking as one steps outwards, but place the left toe down (to enter the Shimata-tachi stance) and open the body to the right. The face is pointed to the enemy, so it should be pointed to the left.

The "opening up" of the body is the main objective here, so do not take the Shimata-tachi stance too suddenly.

The shuto should travel straight ahead. Do this smoothly. If there is excessive strength in the arm, the shuto will not travel straight. This is not the same as a gedan defense.

Be sure to open the body completely. Be careful not to crouch forward or twist the upper body. Move the whole body - not just arms and legs.

Strike using the whole body. Make the shuto "lively" - as in previous examples. Be cautious to not look down at the hands (below) while doing this.

MOVEMENT #19 (1)

MOVEMENT #19 (2)

PIN-AN NIDAN

MOVEMENT #19
Bring the right shuto above the left shuto (towards a line that would connect the feet), step forward with the right foot and punch to the low side with a right shuto and bring back the left shuto to the chest.

Do not move the legs alone - move the body. Be careful not too punch with just a hand; use the shuto.

PIN-AN NIDAN

MOVEMENT #20 (1)

MOVEMENT #20 (2)

PIN-AN NIDAN

MOVEMENT #20
Repeat movement #19 after moving 90° to the right.

Change directions as both shuto and the right foot return from movement #18 to #19. As you are standing up, bring the right leg back to the left leg before kicking. Make sure the body does not move about too much.

PIN-AN NIDAN

MOVEMENT #21 (1)

MOVEMENT #21 (2)

PIN-AN NIDAN

MOVEMENT #21
Move the left foot in front of the right foot, doing a left shuto punch low and taking the stance as in movement #18.

PIN-AN NIDAN

MOVEMENT #22
Withdraw the left foot and return to the posture for preparation. Cleanse the mind and heart as you finish.
(not pictured)

平安(ピンアン)三段

PIN-AN SANDAN

PIN-AN SANDAN

MOVEMENT #1

Turn left, left Nekoashi and do a left jodan defense while bringing the right fist to the chest.

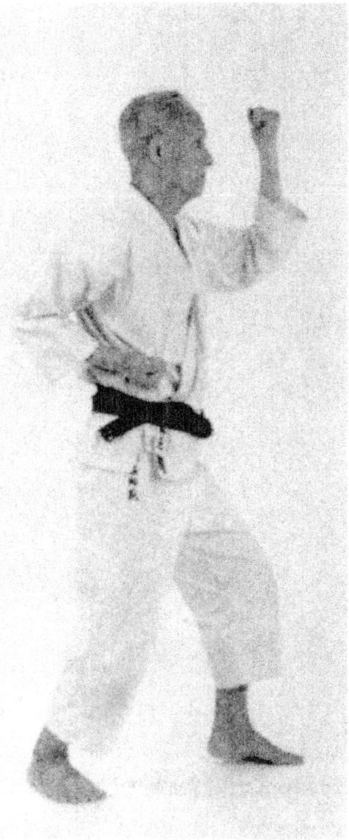

The objective is to completely change the direction to which one faces.

Do not put too much motion into the left arm. The jodan defense must be executed instantaneously. Use the withdrawing of the right fist to assist the left hand's motions.

The left Nekoashi must point straight ahead.

Do not place all of the body's weight on the right foot. Turn with the body.

PIN-AN SANDAN

MOVEMENT #2

PIN-AN SANDAN

MOVEMENT #2

Bring both legs together and do a right jodan block and a left gedan defense simultaneously.

The legs are brought together as a test to see if the left Nekoashi is facing directly forward, as it should be. To stand with both feet together is awkward and unstable. I can not think of any other reason why one would stand in such an awkward way. I still have yet to find a feasible answer to this irregular stance, so I personally, do not know for sure.

PIN-AN SANDAN

MOVEMENT #3

PIN-AN SANDAN

MOVEMENT #3

With the same stance, do a left jodan defense and a right gedan defense simultaneously. The right arm moves inside of the left.

It is difficult to perform both defenses. Do not tense the elbows. Loosen the shoulders and use both defenses correctly.

PIN-AN SANDAN

MOVEMENT #4

PIN-AN SANDAN

MOVEMENT #4
Use the left foot as a pivot, turn around and take a right Nekoashi stance, while doing a right jodan defense and placing the left fist at the chest. Shift quickly and make sure that the Nekoashi is pointing forward. The body must be facing directly ahead. One must not defend when turned only halfway - the same for the Nekoashi. Use the right arm well. For this, pull back on the left fist firmly. Turn with the whole body.

PIN-AN SANDAN

MOVEMENT #5 & #6
Repeat #3 and #2 movements. (not pictured)

PIN-AN SANDAN

MOVEMENT #7

PIN-AN SANDAN

MOVEMENT #7
Turn left 90° left Nekoashi and do a left jodan defense. Bring the right fist to the chest.

PIN-AN SANDAN

MOVEMENT #8
Step forward with the right foot, do a jun-tsuki with a right shuto and bring the left fist back to the chest. Point the small finger down for the shuto. (not pictured)

PIN-AN SANDAN

MOVEMENT #9

PIN-AN SANDAN

MOVEMENT #9
Turn to the left and face behind, while leaning forward - place the right hand palm up against the tail bone and place the left foot at a place appropriate for support.

In response to an opponent who has grasped one's shuto, this stance is taken to minimize any pulling, twisting or other such effects (lean forward to counter the opponent's weight).

Do not bend at the waist. Pull with the whole body, not just the upper body.

PIN-AN SANDAN

MOVEMENT #10

PIN-AN SANDAN

MOVEMENT #10
Leave the right arm as is, turn to the left and take a Shimata-tachi stance and simultaneously pull with the right hand and place it at the chest and then use the left arm to block the opponent's attack. Or, strike the side of the abdomen. The face is pointed to the left, at the opponent. This uses the opponent's strength to one's advantage as the opponent pulls at your arm as in movement #9. Do not lose your balance as you do this, use the waist to push, then pull away.

The right hand is pulled back firmly and not jolted backwards suddenly. Too much strength in the right arm only serves to disrupt your own balance, so do not do this. Remember, kata was created to practice alone, with imaginary enemies.

PIN-AN SANDAN

MOVEMENT#11

PIN-AN SANDAN

MOVEMENT#11

Step forward with the right foot, do a right jun-tsuki and bring the left fist back to the chest.

Pretend to strike at an enemy who is reeling away from you.

Movement #9, #10 and #11 all occur continuously and swiftly. Do not rush these - practice thoroughly. There is a significant difference between rushing movements and doing them swiftly.

PIN-AN SANDAN

MOVEMENT #12

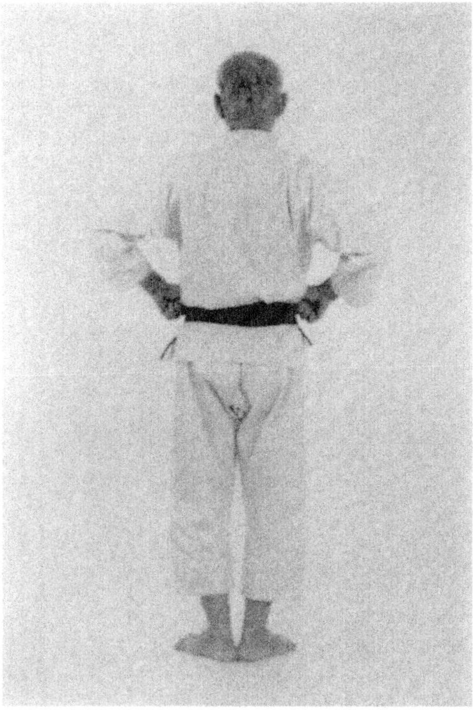

PIN-AN SANDAN

MOVEMENT #12
Pull both feet together, turn around and stand (shift directions to the rear) and place both fists at the waist with the palms pointed behind you. The elbows should not exceed the chest.

Do not rest the thumb on the waist, or bend the waist as the hand rests. Place both fists at the waist level, near one's belt, lightly. This movement tenses the elbows to block an enemy's attack with the elbows. Tense the elbows, but do not place excessive force on the shoulders.

Although the legs are together here, there is really no reason why they ought to be so.

PIN-AN SANDAN

MOVEMENT #13

PIN-AN SANDAN

MOVEMENT #13

Move the right foot forward and take a Shimata-tachi as the body is opened to the left, while raising the right elbow to block and tensing it again at the waist.

Then use the right fist, on the small finger side, to strike at the enemy's lower abdomen and quickly return it to where it was.

One blocks the enemy's attack with the right elbow, but not with the elbow alone - use the force gained from opening the body to the left. As the body opens to the left, the right elbow defends the body from any attacks from the enemy.

Again, use the whole body when using the elbow, or opening up the body to the left. It is important to practice until this habit becomes natural to one's movements.

The last strike is often difficult to accomplish. Collapse the tensed elbow to strike sideways at the enemy's lower abdomen and immediately pull away to tense the elbow again.

If the elbow is too tense, too much strength is placed at the shoulders and it will be difficult to move the arm to strike with. Also, after striking, return the hand while being prepared to defend. Hence do not just move the hand back. Practice this diligently.

PIN-AN SANDAN

MOVEMENT #14

PIN-AN SANDAN

MOVEMENT #14
In a shimata-tachi stance, perform the opposite of movement #13 facing towards the left and facing the head towards the left.

PIN-AN SANDAN

MOVEMENT #15
Repeat as in movement #13. However, leave the sideways punch extended. This is to test if the fist is facing the proper direction in its travel. (not pictured)

PIN-AN SANDAN

MOVEMENT #16
Turn the body to the right, bring the left foot forward and to the right, do a left jun-tsuki and bring the right fist to the chest.

If there is too much strength in the shoulder, one strikes with the force of the arm only. If the elbow remains flexible, more power will develop in the punch naturally. Keep the whole body flexible, yet firm, when striking an enemy. (not pictured)

PIN-AN SANDAN

MOVEMENT #17 (1) **MOVEMENT #17 (2)**

PIN-AN SANDAN

MOVEMENT #17
Shift the right leg around and follow it with the left leg to face the rear and twist only the upper body to pull in the left elbow at the side and punching behind and over the left shoulder. The palm should face down and the forearm should be horizontal.

The previous movement is to defend one's self from an enemy who grabs from behind. But if the opponent is stronger, it may be hard to strike the enemy because the elbow is not free to move. In such cases, there are other actions that can be taken.

The main objective of movement #17 and #18 are to shift the

upper body only, to utilize techniques without moving the lower body.

The waist is essential here - all movements centre around the waist moving. It is easy to strike near the waist because the waist is the centre of one's body weight. The farther the waist is from the punch, the less effective it is, just as in punching over the shoulder. In response to an opponent's attack, the body can not compromise its stability even if one must strike away from his centre of gravity; his waist. It is hence, important to punch with the whole body, in order to not separate a strike, a punch, or a kick from the waist. Excessive strength in the shoulders lifts the waist and makes the body lose its balance. Punch with the twist of the waist as well - it will be more effective. Only use power at the exact moment of contact with the opponent. The punch over the shoulder is not simply just to punch the opponent's face.

PIN-AN SANDAN

MOVEMENT #18

PIN-AN SANDAN

MOVEMENT #18
As in movement #17, punch with the left fist over the right shoulder as one moves towards the right and pulling the right elbow in as the upper body is slightly twisted to the right.

PIN-AN SANDAN

MOVEMENT #19
Straighten the upper body, return the right foot to its normal stance, lower both fists and finish at the posture for preparation. (not pictured)

平安(ピンアン)四段

PIN-AN YONDAN

PIN-AN YONDAN

MOVEMENT #1
Do a left Nekoashi a left jodan defense with the left shuto and place the right hand in front of the forehead.

The head should be turned to the left. (Look at Pin-an Shodan movement #1.)

PIN-AN YONDAN

MOVEMENT #2

PIN-AN YONDAN

MOVEMENT #2
Return the left Nekoashi to its origin and do the reverse of movement #1, to the right this time.

Move the right shuto as if to defend from the enemy.

PIN-AN YONDAN

MOVEMENT #3

PIN-AN YONDAN

MOVEMENT #3
Take a step forward with the left and lower both arms to form an "X" with the right arm on top and look straight ahead.

This is to not defend with crossed arms. It is not impossible to block with both arms, but this is not advantageous, hence, block with one arm and attack with the other. Remember that a kata must be practiced to both the left and to the right.

Thus, the arms are only resting on each other - there should be no excessive strength present.

PIN-AN YONDAN

MOVEMENT #4

PIN-AN YONDAN

MOVEMENT #4
Step forward with the right and do a Nekoashi while doing a right jodan defense and bringing the left fist back to the chest.

The Nekoashi must point straight ahead. The main point here is the defense.

PIN-AN YONDAN

MOVEMENT #5

PIN-AN YONDAN

MOVEMENT #5
Place the legs together, look to the left, bring the right fist to the chest and bring the left forearm to rest slightly against one's lower chest.

Do not force the left fist on to the right fist, lest too much strength will be placed at the left shoulder. Both fists must be prepared to move in any direction at any time.

Both fists should be touching lightly. Never forced against each other. Both fists must remain alive.

PIN-AN YONDAN

MOVEMENT #6

PIN-AN YONDAN

MOVEMENT #6
The left fist performs a left Chudan block, while the left foot does a left side kick.

The left fist must perform the block. Be careful not to do a left jodan defense instead as you are kicking. Never kick with the strength of the leg alone - always use the whole body while kicking and blocking.

Both the kick and defense must occur simultaneously. Later on, one can experiment and alter the defense or the kick, but for now, perform it as I describe.

PIN-AN YONDAN

MOVEMENT #7

PIN-AN YONDAN

MOVEMENT #7
As the left leg comes down, strike with the left elbow straight ahead and place the right elbow into the palm of the left hand. Movement #6 and #7 occur continuously.

Incorporate the twist of the waist into the elbow's contact. Excessive strength makes the elbow rise. The body can not move freely, the upper body lifts (the right foot can not move freely either) and one will tend to crouch forward.

Do not think ahead about the next movement. One kata must never "follow" another kata. Perform every kata as if it were singular and when moving on to the next kata, do not hesitate or place excessive strength anywhere.

The left palm should be fully stretched to receive the elbow and place the thumb securely to not injure it.

The palm should be facing inwards, toward the body, but this is not always the case.

The place where the elbow makes contact should not be too high or low, but about at chest's level.

PIN-AN YONDAN

MOVEMENT #8

PIN-AN YONDAN

MOVEMENT #8

Face the body to the right (forward) and bring the right leg to the left leg, while the head is turned right. Bring the left fist to the chest and the right forearm in front of the upper chest - palm facing down - as in movement #5

Note the similarity to movement #5. The right leg is withdrawn as the body shifts direction, as in Pin-an Sandan, movement #12. In movement #5, notice that one's legs are closed as well. The closed leg probably facilitates a right side kick, in my guess. Remember that as the legs are drawn together, the left leg supports the body. Thus, do not move the leg with the leg alone. Use the whole body to "move" the leg.

PIN-AN YONDAN

MOVEMENT #9	MOVEMENT #10
	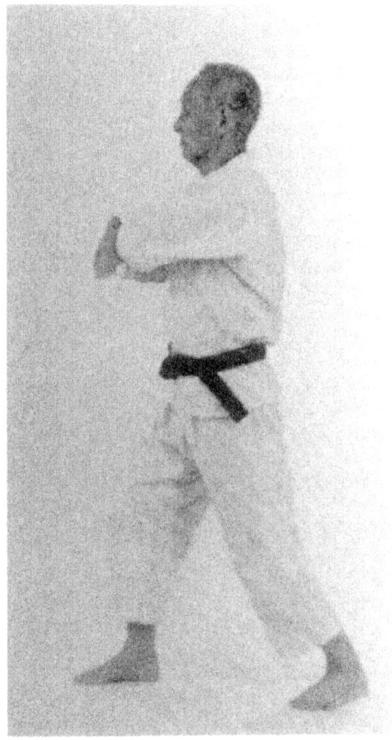

PIN-AN YONDAN

MOVEMENT #9 & #10
Do the reverse actions of movement #6 and #7 continuously.

PIN-AN YONDAN

MOVEMENT#11

PIN-AN YONDAN

MOVEMENT#11
The right leg is the pivot - move the left foot slightly and face the left while twisting the upper body to the left and rotating the right arm as if to do a side defense and pretend to grab the opponent's wrist. The left hand, in a shuto, should be placed in front of the forehead.

Unless the upper body is twisted slightly, the body will lose its balance. The right hand's small finger should be pointed down and pretend to grab the enemy's wrist from the side, not from above or below. However, the left hand does not do the same. Maintain the left hand in the shuto. Do not bend the left wrist as it is forming a shuto. A good shuto can not be executed if the wrist is not kept straight.

PIN-AN YONDAN

MOVEMENT #12 (1)

MOVEMENT #12 (2)

PIN-AN YONDAN

MOVEMENT #12

Do a front kick with the right foot and follow through by striking the opponent's face with the back of the right hand, then do a left Nekoashi and bring that left foot beside the right heel. Bring down the left arm as if to strike down at an enemy's attack and quickly pull it back and place it beside the chest.

When moving the foot, use the strength of the whole body. Do not extend the right knee too far forward, or the body will lose its balance. Move with the body and stand with the body.

The right arm should be held lightly, but become forceful when the right fist strikes the opponent and simultaneously, the left arm must be pulled in towards one's chest firmly and swiftly. Maintain an equal distribution of strength to the body's left and right through all actions.

As the body moves forward, the left arm must defend the whole body. Take caution to any attack to your right side of the body. When the left leg does a Nekoashi, the body's weight is distributed equally on both legs. Do not support the body with the right leg alone. It will become difficult to turn the whole body completely. Practice diligently. Movement #11 and #12 occur continuously.

PIN-AN YONDAN

MOVEMENT #13

Use the right foot as a pivot, and turn to the rear 225° do a left Nekoashi a left jodan defense and bring the right hand beside the chest.

The essential point is the rotating of the body. Take care in doing the defense as well. (not pictured)

MOVEMENT #14

PIN-AN YONDAN

MOVEMENT #14
Do a right front kick and follow through with a right punch and a left punch.

Do not kick and punch with the legs or arms alone. Do these with the body. Punch accurately and use the gyaku-tsuki stance in this movement.

Movement #13 and #14 are done continuously.

MOVEMENT #15

PIN-AN YONDAN

MOVEMENT #15
Turn to the right 90° do a right Nekoashi a right jodan defense and bring the left fist back to the chest.

PIN-AN YONDAN

MOVEMENT #16

PIN-AN YONDAN

MOVEMENT #16
Do a left front kick and follow with a left punch and a right punch.

Movement #15 and #16 occur continuously.

PIN-AN YONDAN

MOVEMENT #17

PIN-AN YONDAN

MOVEMENT #17
Move the left foot 45° to the left, do a Nekoashi and a left jodan defense. The right fist blocks the enemy's attack and is placed by the chest's side.

Defend with the Mahanmi stance and raise the right forearm slightly to block the enemy's attack. Lower the body if it is appropriate to do so.

PIN-AN YONDAN

MOVEMENT #18 & #19

PIN-AN YONDAN

MOVEMENT #18 & #19
Do as in movement #17 to the right and left, alternately.

As in Pin-an Shodan movement #9 and #10 make sure the body and shoulder rotate 90° only.

PIN-AN YONDAN

MOVEMENT #20

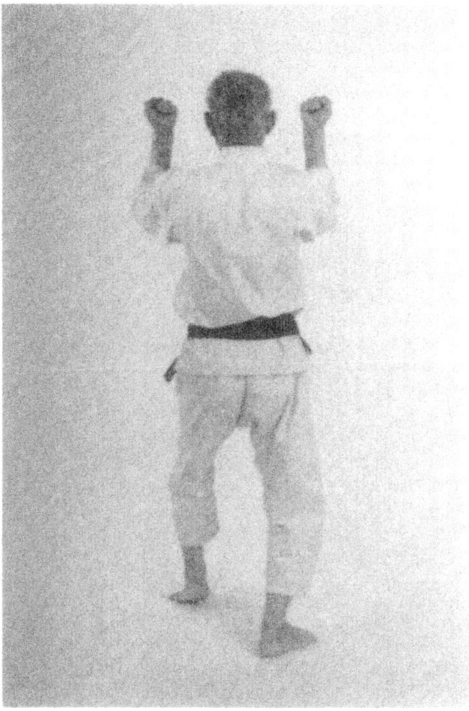

PIN-AN YONDAN

MOVEMENT #20

Open the body to the left and move the left Nekoashi to face the body straight ahead and simultaneously do a right jodan defense. Leave the left arm in a defense.

Look at Pin-an Sandan, movement #2 as reference.

Too much strength in the shoulder will push both right and left defenses outwards, so use caution.

Use the whole body as the right jodan defense is performed. This right defense should occur to the opponent's inner side.

PIN-AN YONDAN

MOVEMENT #21

PIN-AN YONDAN

MOVEMENT #21
Pull both arms back firmly (at about 35° from the body) and kick upwards with the right knee.

The knee should move quickly and with force. Do not extend the arms too wide, or this will make you lose your balance. The enemy may fall on you as you move your arms to regain your balance.

Also, if too much strength is placed in the arms, this will weaken your knee and make you lose your balance. The body must maintain its stability, always.

Both palms should travel along the center of the body.

Pretend as if you are pulling at the opponent's arm. In other situations, one may grab the enemy's collar, neck, ears, hair and so on.

Also, the knee can be used when one grapples with the opponent. Some common targets are the head, chest, lower stomach and thighs.

PIN-AN YONDAN

MOVEMENT #22

PIN-AN YONDAN

MOVEMENT #22
As the right foot is lowered, turn around (225° to the rear) and do a Mahanmi - left Nekoashi as the left arm does a side block and grabs that attack with the palm facing down. The right arm, similarly, does a Chudan block and grabs that attack with the palm faced down.

The defense occurs as in movement #17.

The defense is essential here. This defense is very difficult, so practice thoroughly. The left arm can not bend at the elbows as it is trying to grab the enemy's attacking arm. The same applies for the right elbow as it is attempting to grab (place strength in the hands here) the enemy's attack and grab from above.

The left arm (jodan defense) originates from below the right arm (Chudan defense) to defend (the right arm above the left arm).

Left and right defenses occur simultaneously.

There should not be too much space between the right palm and left elbow. Too much strength in the shoulder will cause this to occur.

PIN-AN YONDAN

MOVEMENT #23

PIN-AN YONDAN

MOVEMENT #23
Lower the left heel, raise the right toes and place the heel right diagonally ahead, then do a right Nekoashi while pulling in the left foot and looking in the same direction - simultaneously do a right jodan and left Chudan defense, as in movement #22.

Beginners always have problems here. Do not move the body with the feet alone. The body moves the body and the Nekoashi is only to assist the body in this shifting. Any movements of the Nekoashi must be performed with the body.

PIN-AN YONDAN

MOVEMENT #24

Move the left foot diagonally backwards (in line with the right) and return to the posture for preparation. (not pictured)

平安(ピンアン)五段

PIN-AN GODAN

PIN-AN GODAN

MOVEMENT #1
Same as Pin-an Sandan movement #1.

The body's rotation is the main focus.

One may perform a defense in the Mahanmi stance. However, both feet must be in the gyaku-tsuki stance as well, so this must be practiced diligently.

PIN-AN GODAN

MOVEMENT #2
With a left Nekoashi, punch with the right fist and bring the left fist beside the chest.

When striking with the arms only, one will see that the Nekoashi will tend to point diagonally. Make sure to punch with the whole body. In a Mahanmi stance, alter the Nekoashi slightly to do a Naihanchi stance.

Movement #1 and #2 occur continuously.

PIN-AN GODAN

MOVEMENT #3

PIN-AN GODAN

MOVEMENT #3
Look to the right, as the right foot is drawn to the left foot and the body turns forward. Bring the right fist to the chest and the left arm in front of the chest, but with a little space in between.

Place a little space between the forearm and the chest. The left arm may touch the body slightly, but it is preferable to keep them apart. This is similar to Pin-an Yondan, movement #5. Try to not close the legs together as the right foot is drawn. Also, this movement shall be done smoothly; in one continuous "flow." All actions may be referred to movement #24 of Pin-an Yondan.

PIN-AN GODAN

MOVEMENT #4

MOVEMENT #5

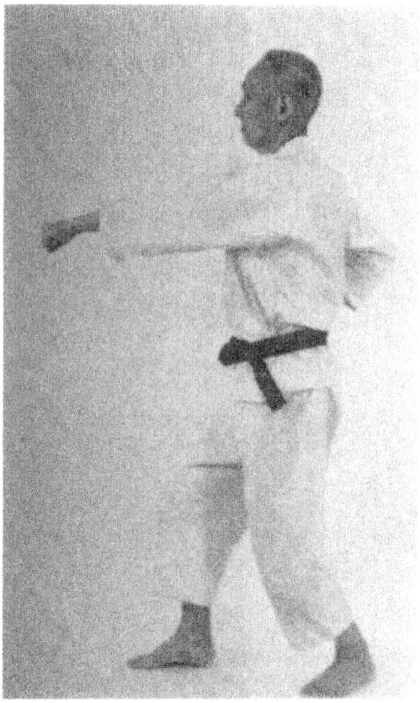

PIN-AN GODAN

MOVEMENT #4 & #5
Do the opposite of movement #1 and #2 continuously.

PIN-AN GODAN

MOVEMENT #6

PIN-AN GODAN

MOVEMENT #6
As a reverse of movement #3, pull the left leg towards the right leg and face forward (the head is forward as well) with the left fist by the chest and the right fist in front of the chest.

In movement #3 and #6, do not raise the elbow while moving. If the elbow, hand, or foot is not prepared to alter its course while moving, this kata is "dead" and pointless. Remember to keep the movements "alive."

PIN-AN GODAN

MOVEMENT #7

PIN-AN GODAN

MOVEMENT #7
Move the right leg forward and do a Nekoashi as in Pin-an Yondan, movement #4.

MOVEMENT #8

PIN-AN GODAN

MOVEMENT #8
Take a step forward with the left and do as in Pin-an Yondan, movement #3.

PIN-AN GODAN

MOVEMENT #9

PIN-AN GODAN

MOVEMENT #9

Both hands are in a shuto and simultaneously perform a jodan defense.

Do not defend with the "cross" of the arms. Refer to Pin-an Yondan, movement #3.

Do not place one arm firmly against the other. If the opponent is stronger than you, you will not be able to raise both arms.

As both arms are raised, turn both palms slightly toward the body (without lifting the waist - keep both shuto almost diagonal) and then do a jodan defense. Do not place excessive strength in the arms.

After defending, if strength remains unnecessarily, both wrists tend to bend. Prepare to block, defend, attack or perform any other action with both arms after defending.

Instead of doing the left and right defenses separately, this seemed more feasible. However, both the left and right defenses must be flawless for this defense to succeed.

PIN-AN GODAN

MOVEMENT #10

PIN-AN GODAN

MOVEMENT #10
Face the right palm upwards and defend the enemy's Chudan attack while the left palm faces downwards to do a Chudan defense. Cross both arms with left above and the right below.

The defense does not occur with both arms. The left and right arms perform simultaneous defenses, together.

Both arms are horizontal, but they only touch slightly.

The defense becomes flawed if the left arm is punched by the right arm. This occurs if one tries to block with only the strength of both arms and not the whole body.

Also, if there is too much power in the shoulders, the elbows become extended and the arms rest on each other.

Be careful not to bend both wrists as one defends. Both defenses should block with the middle of the forarms. Take care not to raise the elbows.

Both the left and right defenses are separate defenses; not together.

PIN-AN GODAN

MOVEMENT#11
Punch with the left and draw the right fist to the chest.

The left punch is thrown from where one stands. Pull back the right fist to assist this action. (not pictured)

PIN-AN GODAN

MOVEMENT #12
Step forward with the right foot and do a right jun-tsuki and bring the left fist back to the chest.

Do not think of the next movement that follows, or this movement will become compromised in its execution. Remember to use "lively" movements for every movement.

Movements #8, #9, #10 and #11 are to the left; #8, #9, #10 and #12 are to the right - hence, they are separate, yet continuous.

Movement #8 to #12 are performed continuously and smoothly. (not pictured)

PIN-AN GODAN

MOVEMENT #13

PIN-AN GODAN

MOVEMENT #13
Move the right leg backward and turn to the left to do a Shimata - tachi (turn 270°), turn the head right and do a right gedan defense.

Use the body to move the body, or the left knee will move up and down and the defense will become weak.

Move as if to "pull in" the enemy's attack and let the body "pull" the legs along.

The right fist should come near the right ear (the palm should be pointed to the rear) to do the defense.

PIN-AN GODAN

MOVEMENT #14

PIN-AN GODAN

MOVEMENT #14

As the left foot is drawn back to stand, turn the head to the left, do a left Chudan block and bring the right fist back to the chest. Do not pull the leg, but move it with the whole body.

Do not just extend the left arm to the left, but incorporate a twist into it. Too much strength in the left fist will not allow you to move the body and do the defense at the same time. The body's shifting, the left defense and the shifting of the right hand and head must occur at the same time. The left fist should not move around so much (keep the palm faced downwards) as it defends. Move the right fist to counter the left fist's movements. The body will stand at balance only if all movements occur simultaneously and equally.

PIN-AN GODAN

MOVEMENT #15

PIN-AN GODAN

MOVEMENT #15
Take a step forward to the left with the right foot and do a right elbow strike.

Refer to Pin-an Yondan, movement #7.

MOVEMENT #16

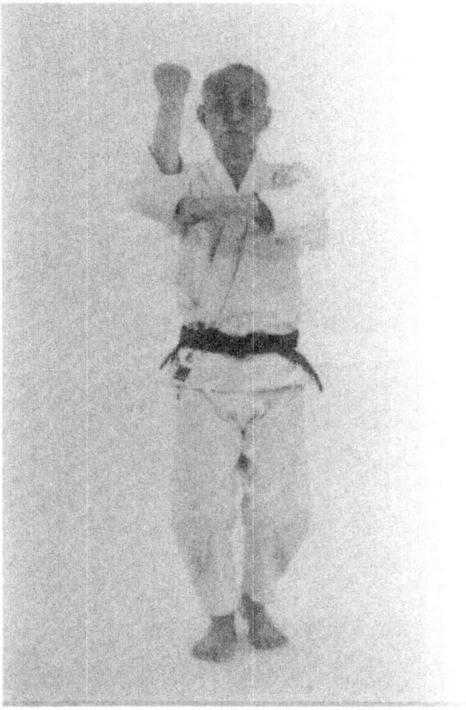

PIN-AN GODAN

MOVEMENT #16

Do a right jodan defense and bring the left fist (palm downward) in front of the chest and quickly move the left foot behind and to the left of the right heel (Nekoashi). As one defends from a jodan attack from the front, withdraw quickly towards the rear.

Do not skip with the left foot as it is withdrawn. Take care not to extend the right knee, crouch forward, or stand erect. Perform every action using the whole body. Refer to Pin-an Yondan, movement #12. Keep the body facing forward; do not become right-Hanmi. The left fist is held relatively high. It may touch the right elbow slightly.

PIN-AN GODAN

MOVEMENT #17

PIN-AN GODAN

MOVEMENT #17
Move the body (the enemy is at left) and the left foot to the right and do a right jodan defense immediately followed by a punch to the enemy's face (palm facing up). Turn the head to the left and look at the enemy behind you. Bring the left fist, palm down, in front of the chest.

Turn the body completely to place the enemy at the sides. If only the legs are used, the turn will be incomplete and one's waist will become pointed at the opponent.

Take a wide stance and move the feet (to point properly) as well. Point the left foot slightly outward. Body's balance will be lost if the feet are not stable. Remember to see the enemy behind you, too.

The right punch is done with the whole body. If punched with the arm alone, one's upper body will rise. Lower the left elbow as the punch is thrown and prepare to react for any surprise attacks.

PIN-AN GODAN

MOVEMENT #18
Jump over, as the enemy on the left attempts to trip you, face opposite and cross both arms - right on top - to do a gedan - block and look to the front.

When jumping, jump high.

When landing, both feet should be used to keep the body straight and low. Do not look down. Constantly stare at the enemy's face while jumping.

The left leg should be behind the right leg and both knees are to be flexible. The objective here is also to strengthen the ankles.

When both feet are not used, one tends to crouch forward at landing. Use both feet, to be able to react to the next attack.

The gedan block is formed as you jump up and defense occurs simultaneously as you land.

Remember to face the opposite direction as you land. Never forget to imagine the enemy in all of these movements. In some situations, one may land to place the enemy at the left, to one's right hand side. However, this may not be too wise.

This movement reinforces a jump, a shift of the body, as well as a gedan block. Instead of the block, one may chose to kick or punch as well, if appropriate. However, I choose to block in this kata.

From movement #13 to #18, imagine that there are opponents to both the front and rear, so perform these continuously, also.

PIN-AN GODAN

MOVEMENT #19

Take a step to the right with the right foot, take a jun-tsuki stance, do a right jodan defense and bring the left arm in front of the chest.

Defend after twisting the waist. Refer to Pin-an Shodan movement #20. Turn the body completely to the right.

It is easy to not stand completely because one moves from a low posture. Leave plenty of space between both feet. Do not stand with the legs alone; stand with the whole body. (not pictured)

PIN-AN GODAN

MOVEMENT #20

PIN-AN GODAN

MOVEMENT #20
Turn the body left and bend diagonally right while placing the right arm high and left arm low and turning the palms inwards, as if to block an attack from behind. Turn the body completely, as in movement #17. To practice this movement, turn facing forward in movement #19.

Do not destabilize the lower body by placing too much strength in the shoulder, or raising the right arm too high. As long as the whole body is standing and erect, it facilitates reaction to the enemy's next attack. Do not place strength in both arms. The right arm is bent diagonally, with the upper arm at shoulder level and the left arm should be held parallel to this arm.

PIN-AN GODAN

MOVEMENT #21

PIN-AN GODAN

MOVEMENT #21
Do the same movement in the opposite direction. Do all the movements exactly, as in movement #20, but rotate the right leg 45° to the right this time.

This movement is repetitive from left to right, but be sure to stand straight and upright when the legs are drawn together. Pull the legs together with the whole body.

PIN-AN GODAN

MOVEMENT #22

At the finish, draw the right leg and return to the posture for preparation. (not pictured)

PIN-AN GODAN

MOVEMENT #23

Move the left foot first, then the right, open the fists and return to the stance at start. (not pictured)

公相君（クーシャンクー）

KUSHAN-KU

KUSHAN-KU

This kata was founded 200 years ago, in Shina, by a person named Kushanku. Presently, there are many forms to this kata. It is simply called "Kushanku."

This kata rotates the body forward, back, left and right, with both hands and feet. It is similar to Pin-an in that sense. Once one masters Pin-an, it would make sense to study this kata next. One must be reminded that this kata moves swiftly and in all directions. Every single movement must be correct and quickly executed. This kata places the shifting of the body as its main objective.

HOW TO STAND
Same as in Pin-an.

KUSHAN-KU

POSTURE FOR PREPARATION

Open, the left foot first, followed by the right foot and place the left hand above the right hand and place them in front of the body.

Do not cross the thumbs, or push the hands against each other.

This can be seen in jui jitsu as well; it protects the body but prepares one to strike also. **Kushanku** does look "fancy" as it involves large movements of the limbs. However, this is not for show or other such immature interpretations. Remember that the kata expresses what one is thinking in his mind. The kata is not a dance, or an exercise routine. These are "igata," the kata is not. The kata must remain "living," not "dead."

KUSHAN-KU

MOVEMENT #1 (1)

MOVEMENT #1 (2)

KUSHAN-KU

MOVEMENT #1

Raise both hands (not straight up but forward and up), make both hands into shuto, separate, make a circle and return them to their original position with the palms facing forward and place the left ring and small fingers over the right ring and small fingers, almost touching. Do not look at the fingers, but straight ahead at the enemy.

This movement is done silently and smoothly. In the shuto, do not press the right hand into the left palm. Hold the hands so that both ring fingers barely touch each other.

Extend both arms fully as the arms do a circle and do not push them backwards. When seen from the front, one should observe a circle.

Keep the eyes focused on the enemy and do not look up, or at

KUSHAN-KU

MOVEMENT #1 (3)

the hands as they move.

This movement illustrates that you have no weapon in your hands, as well as the cyclical nature of the world and peace. Hence, the required smoothness when performing the circle.

KUSHAN-KU

MOVEMENT #2
Do a left Nekoashi to the left and do a left shuto jodan defense while bringing the right shuto (palm facing up) in front of the chest. The head should be turned to the left.

KUSHAN-KU

MOVEMENT #3

KUSHAN-KU

MOVEMENT #3
Return the left foot to its origin and do the same of movement #2, to the right.

Refer to Pin-an Yondan, movement #2. The left shuto is brought in front of the chest.

KUSHAN-KU

MOVEMENT #4

KUSHAN-KU

MOVEMENT #4
Return the right Nekoashi to its origin and do as in Pin-an Yondan movement #5 and point the head straight ahead.

KUSHAN-KU

MOVEMENT #5

KUSHAN-KU

MOVEMENT #5
With the left arm, block the enemy's Chudan strike to the side.

As the left arm blocks, the fist is lowered slightly.

KUSHAN-KU

MOVEMENT #6

KUSHAN-KU

MOVEMENT #6

Maintain the stance and punch with the right fist (legs do not move). Withdraw the left fist and place beside the chest.

Movement #5 and #6 occur continuously.

KUSHAN-KU

MOVEMENT #7

KUSHAN-KU

MOVEMENT #7
Move the left foot wide and turn the upper body to the left and do a right jodan defense. The face keeps looking forward (to the right).

The body moves the left foot. This is to move the body to avoid an enemy's strike. Plant the left toe firmly and do a defense at the same time the upper body is turned (variation of Sei-shan).

Refer to Pin-an Shodan, movement #18. As the body moves to the left and then turns, the defense must occur simultaneously. Do not place excessive power in the shoulders.

KUSHAN-KU

MOVEMENT #8

KUSHAN-KU

MOVEMENT #8
Withdraw the left foot and punch with the left fist while bringing the right fist beside the chest.

Withdraw with the whole body, not just the leg.

Movements #7 and #8 are continuous.

KUSHAN-KU

MOVEMENT #9

KUSHAN-KU

MOVEMENT #9
Move the body to the right, step forward with the right foot, do a left jodan defense with the left arm and turn the upper body to the right. The upper body faces right, but the face is turned to the left.

In movement #7 and #9, be careful no to crouch forward as the upper body is turned.

KUSHAN-KU

MOVEMENT #10

KUSHAN-KU

MOVEMENT #10
Do as in Pin-an Shodan, movement #7 (do not lower the right fist before blocking). Place the left fist at the chest and look to the right (behind).

One tends to place excessive motion on the body, if the left leg is placed beside the right leg before doing the side kick. Place the left leg at a location that makes the right side kick easier, because the defense with the right arm and the kick must occur simultaneously.

KUSHAN-KU

MOVEMENT#11

KUSHAN-KU

MOVEMENT#11
Do as in Pin-an Shodan, movement #8

Movement #9, #10 and #11 occur continuously.

MOVEMENT #12

MOVEMENT #13

KUSHAN-KU

MOVEMENT #12, #13 & #14
Movement #12, #13 and #14 are identical to Pin-an Shodan, movement #9, #10 and #11.

Be careful in doing the right shuto attack, as it can move the body too far to the left.

MOVEMENT #14

KUSHAN-KU

MOVEMENT #15

KUSHAN-KU

MOVEMENT #15
Turn to the left by moving the left foot backwards and do as in Pin-an Yodan, movement #11.

Use the right leg as a pivot and lower the body slightly.

KUSHAN-KU

MOVEMENT #16

KUSHAN-KU

MOVEMENT #16
Do a right kick forward.

Do not take your eyes off the opponent. If the eye looks elsewhere, one risks missing with the kick and lowering the body too much.

KUSHAN-KU

MOVEMENT #17

KUSHAN-KU

MOVEMENT #17
To respond to an attack from behind (if the enemy is using a staff), place the enemy to your left, lower the kicked leg, bend at the knee and lower the body while placing the right fist in front of the forehead and place the left arm low, towards the opponent. Keep the eyes fixed onto the opponent.

Do not think about the next movement, as this will cause a loss of balance. Too much space between the feet will cause the body to falter as well. One is not escaping from the enemy's attack, but avoiding it to retaliate immediately afterwards. Hence, after kicking the enemy in front, turn around and avoid the attack from the enemy behind you with this movement. Move with the whole body; never the legs alone. By moving with the whole body, one is then able to retaliate with the next movement.

Place the opponent to the left, bend the right knee and lower the body. Point the right toe slightly inward. The outer side of the left foot will naturally lift. Be careful to not lose the body's balance by turning the head. Do not place too much of the body's weight on the right foot, lest it will be fixed to the floor.

When kicking, rotate the right arm as you raise it to the head. This accounts for the body's loss of balance as the right leg is kicked outwards. Lower the whole body quickly and the right arm shall follow, naturally. Keep your stance low.

KUSHAN-KU

MOVEMENT #18

KUSHAN-KU

MOVEMENT #18
Extend the right arm to block an enemy's attack. At the same time, bend the left elbow and cross it with the right arm by placing it over the right arm.

Twist both forearms sufficiently in their travel. Do not look at the hands while they are in motion.

KUSHAN-KU

MOVEMENT #19

KUSHAN-KU

MOVEMENT #19
Pull back the left foot to stand up, pull back the right fist firmly to the chest and simultaneously punch with the left fist towards the left.

Stand sideways and face left. As the leg is being withdrawn, punch forcefully at the enemy's lower abdomen. Punching the enemy's lower abdomen has the best chance of collapsing the enemy's balance in this situation. When standing upright, stand with the whole body and pull the leg with the body.

Movement #15 to #19 must be continuous, correct and swift. Movement #18 and #19 are not performed slowly as I sometimes have seen, but swiftly. Do not use excessive strength or force here. Take caution and practice.

KUSHAN-KU

MOVEMENT #20

KUSHAN-KU

MOVEMENT #20
Do as in movement #15, to the left.

MOVEMENT #21

MOVEMENT #22

KUSHAN-KU

MOVEMENT #21, #22, #23 & #24

Movement #21 to #24 are identical to movement #16 to #19.

Movement #20 to #24 are done accurately, smoothly and continuously.

MOVEMENT #23

KUSHAN-KU

MOVEMENT #24

MOVEMENT #25

KUSHAN-KU

MOVEMENT #25
Turn the body to the left and pull the left foot in as one takes the stance as in Pin-an Yondan, movement #5. The face turns to the left.

KUSHAN-KU

MOVEMENT #26 - #30
Movement #26 to #30 are identical to Pin-an Yondan, movement #6 to #10.

MOVEMENT #28

MOVEMENT #26

MOVEMENT #27

MOVEMENT #29

MOVEMENT #30

KUSHAN-KU

MOVEMENT #31

KUSHAN-KU

MOVEMENT #31
Turn the body quickly to the left, left Nekoashi and take a Mahanmi - stance towards the rear and do a left shuto jodan defense.

KUSHAN-KU

MOVEMENT #32

KUSHAN-KU

MOVEMENT #32
Step left diagonally forward with the right foot (95° to the right diagonally), do a right Nekoashi with a Mahanmi stance and do a right shuto jodan defense.

KUSHAN-KU

MOVEMENT #33

KUSHAN-KU

MOVEMENT #33
Turn right and place the right foot 135° behind, do a Nekoashi and in a Mahanmi stance, do a right shuto jodan defense.

KUSHAN-KU

MOVEMENT #34

KUSHAN-KU

MOVEMENT #34
Move the left foot diagonally forward (45° left diagonally from the right foot), do a left Nekoashi and in a Mahanmi stance, do a left shuto jodan defense.

KUSHAN-KU

MOVEMENT #35

KUSHAN-KU

MOVEMENT #35
Move the left foot towards the left and do as in movement #15, 45° to the left.

KUSHAN-KU

MOVEMENT #36 (1)

KUSHAN-KU

MOVEMENT #36
Do as in Pin-an Yondan, movement #12.

Movement #35 and #36 occur continuously.

While doing the Kushanku do not rush or else one movement will rush into another and the flow of movements will be lost.

The same applies to this movement, as it is no exception to that fact. There is a difference between rushed and swift, erred and accurate. Do not think of the next movement as one is doing another - concentrate on the movement being performed. Hence, it is important to practice so that the flow of movements occurs naturally. With increased practice comes increased fluidity of the movements.

KUSHAN-KU

MOVEMENT #36 (2)

I suppose it is similar to an individual being able to walk in his house without the lights on. And one must not forget the kata, either. In the beginning only practice while thinking about the next movement, however, as time progresses, this practice must be discontinued.

KUSHAN-KU

MOVEMENT #37

Jump backwards and take the jun-tsuki stance while holding the left fist at the chest and doing a right jodan defense.

Do not jump, with the legs alone; move the whole body. Be careful of the space between your feet - not too narrow, not too wide; and do not bend at the knees. The right defense occurs as the body is descending; hence, defend as the body lands.

MOVEMENT #38 (1)

MOVEMENT #38 (2)

KUSHAN-KU

MOVEMENT #38
Punch with the left fist, then the right.

Movement #37 and #38 are continuous. Both punches strike only one target. Do not rush between the two punches and use the whole body as the punches strike - never the strength of the arms alone.

Incorporate the twist of the waist into the punches. Do not use excessive strength before and after the punches' contact.

KUSHAN-KU

MOVEMENT #39

KUSHAN-KU

MOVEMENT #39
Use the left leg as a pivot to turn left and raise the right leg, bend at the knee, to hit the area near the right knee with the left hand and perform a shuto afterwards and place it above the knee with the small finger side downwards; simultaneously, with the palm facing upwards, point the right arm straight ahead so that the small finger of the right hand almost touches the middle and ring fingers of the left hand and look straight ahead.

The objective of this movement is to kick, by making the attack of the enemy in front coincide with the enemy from the rear's attack (which may be a kick, a punch, or a swing of a staff). This movement uses many actions; it is one of the best movements. And, instead of kicking, I suppose one could punch instead, but I have chosen to use a kick here.

One may deceive an enemy by making a loud noise as he hits his knee, however, the right punch and the left shuto must make contact nevertheless. Take care so that these actions both sufficiently strike the enemy.

If one performs the above actions hurriedly, his upper body may fall forward, or he may look downward, or his hands may miss their intended target. Movement #39 must be diligently and accurately practiced.

KUSHAN-KU

MOVEMENT #40

KUSHAN-KU

MOVEMENT #40

Lean forward low and stand on the toes of the right foot, supporting the body by placing the fingers on the ground. Naturally, the left foot supports the body on its toes only.

This movement avoids any subsequent high attacks from an enemy who is behind. Do not move the left leg back after going down. The left leg should not have to be moved, as long as it is not moved when the body goes down towards the ground. The fingers only lightly support the body's weight. The fingers should point slightly inward. This should prevent the elbows from being injured, if the body falls further accidentally.

KUSHAN-KU

MOVEMENT #41

KUSHAN-KU

MOVEMENT #41
Look to the rear as you spring to your feet, draw the left foot and do a Nekoashi and in a Mahanmi stance, do a left shuto defense.

Do not spring up with the hands or the right leg alone. Rise with the whole body. The strength of the left ankle must not be ignored here.

Movement #39, #40 and #41 occur continuously and swiftly.

KUSHAN-KU

MOVEMENT #42

KUSHAN-KU

MOVEMENT #42
Move forward one step, do a right Nekoashi and do a right shuto defense in a Mahanmi stance.

KUSHAN-KU

MOVEMENT #43

KUSHAN-KU

MOVEMENT #43

Using the right leg as a pivot, turn to the rear 270° do a left Nekoashi form both hands into a shuto and do a left jodan defense. Place the right fist by the chest.

Refer to Pin-an Sandan, movement #1. Remember to turn the body completely and then doing the defense.

KUSHAN-KU

MOVEMENT #44

KUSHAN-KU

MOVEMENT #44
In that stance, punch with the right fist and pull in the left fist beside the chest.

KUSHAN-KU

MOVEMENT #45

KUSHAN-KU

MOVEMENT #45
As one turns around backwards, jump forward on the right foot, followed by the left foot and do a right Nekoashi with a right jodan defense.

This movement requires one to turn to the rear, jump forward and defend - however, the main objective here is the changing of direction faced, as well as the Nekoashi and defense which follow.

MOVEMENT #46 (1)

MOVEMENT #46 (2)

KUSHAN-KU

MOVEMENT #46

From that stance, do a left punch followed by a right punch.

KUSHAN-KU

MOVEMENT #47

KUSHAN-KU

MOVEMENT #47

Do a right jodan defense with the right arm and simultaneously do a right side kick with the right leg. The head is turned to the right.

Kick to the right immediately after the Nekoashi. If the Nekoashi is not performed well, this kick can not be executed.

KUSHAN-KU

MOVEMENT #48

KUSHAN-KU

MOVEMENT #48
Lower the right leg beside the left leg and open the left leg to do a left Nekoashi to the left; form shuto with both hands and in a Mahanmi stance, do a left shuto jodan defense.

Movement #47 and #48 are done continuously. Imagine the enemy to be at the sides of one's body here.

KUSHAN-KU

MOVEMENT #49 (1)

MOVEMENT #49 (2)

KUSHAN-KU

MOVEMENT #49
Block an opponent's Chudan attack by moving the left forearm, palm facing down, to the side and take a step forward with the right foot and do a jun-tsuki with a right shuto. The right shuto will travel above the left forearm.

Attempt to defend with the left elbow rather than the forearm. Defend at the same time the left heel is lowered (keep the waist down and the forearm horizontal); the right shuto should not interfere with any of the above actions and strike quickly.

MOVEMENT #50 (1)

MOVEMENT #50 (2)

KUSHAN-KU

MOVEMENT #50
Lower the right shoulder slightly and turn the body left to bring the left foot towards the enemy and do a Shimata-tachi stance (place the enemy to the left) and simultaneously, pull the right hand firmly toward the chest and with the left fist, block the enemy's Chudan attack to the side. The head is turned to the left.

Gyaku-te is used to not counter the enemy's strength, but to use it to one's advantage. The body will collapse if the foot is used as a pivot. Hence, lower the shoulder as if to carry one's body weight towards the opponent. If one turns while the right arm is outstretched and the body straight, this will go against the enemy's force. Be careful not to counter the force of the enemy's attack directly.

KUSHAN-KU

MOVEMENT #51

KUSHAN-KU

MOVEMENT #51

With the Shimata-tachi stance, advance to the left (towards the enemy) and using the back of the left fist, strike downwards at the opponent's face.

KUSHAN-KU

MOVEMENT #52

KUSHAN-KU

MOVEMENT #52
Turn the body to the left and do as in movement #27.

Movement #50, #51 and #52 occur continuously.

Turn the body completely forward. Be careful that the upper body does not turn left by itself, or you miss hitting with the elbow.

KUSHAN-KU

MOVEMENT #53

KUSHAN-KU

MOVEMENT #53
Draw the right leg and open the body to the right, turn right and place the enemy to one's right side and do a Chudan defense to the right with the right arm, while erecting the left arm vertically (elbow below the shoulder, palms facing inward) and turning the head to the right.

Imagine that an enemy is about to strike at one's back from behind for this movement. Do not pull the right leg; pull the whole body.

KUSHAN-KU

MOVEMENT #54

KUSHAN-KU

MOVEMENT #54
Move the left foot to the right, face the opposite direction and extend the left arm with palms forward and strike downward - stopping at the middle of the body and taking a Shimata-tachi stance, while moving the right arm above and to the right as the left arm in movement #53. Face forward.

This movement defends from an opponent who follows with a kick. This kata has one "open" the body, before he defends from an opponent's kick from the right (which is actually left because the body shifts before it defends). However, face forward nevertheless because this movement is to practice "opening" the body and defending; hence, there is no need to think ahead. Remember that kata is averaged to the left and right for weight, strength and so on. In movement #55, one may do the gedan block with the right arm as well, when it can be done with the left from the Shimata-tachi stance.

When striking with the left arm, do not let the forearm "fall" forward to defend. Let the arm fall to the left, outer side in order to defend properly. The fist held above should be ready to move in any direction, to do anything. Do not place too much strength in the left arm, lest one risks making the other arm unable to react immediately, or worse, even to move. Movement #53 and #54 are done continuously.

KUSHAN-KU

MOVEMENT #55

KUSHAN-KU

MOVEMENT #55
Lower the right arm to the right and extend it to do a gedan-block, then place it underneath the left arm. Both palms face forward.

KUSHAN-KU

MOVEMENT #56

KUSHAN-KU

MOVEMENT #56
Simultaneously, do a shuto - jodan defense to the left and the right.

Identical to Pin-an Godan, movement #9 in reasoning.

KUSHAN-KU

MOVEMENT #57

KUSHAN-KU

MOVEMENT #57
Move the left foot 270° to the right and take a jun-tsuki stance.

Refer to Pin-an Nidan, movement #3; do not turn with the leg only. If both shuto contain excessive strength, the body will not move smoothly. Place almost no strength in both arms while they are raised.

KUSHAN-KU

MOVEMENT #58

KUSHAN-KU

MOVEMENT #58
Simultaneously, use both forearms to defend from the opponent's Chudan attack. Form fists with both hands, with the small finger pointed down.

Lower both arms horizontally to defend properly.

KUSHAN-KU

MOVEMENT #59 (1) **MOVEMENT #59 (2)**

KUSHAN-KU

MOVEMENT #59
Jump, kick forward and kick with the right foot while airborne (two kicks) and as the body lands (stands for jun-tsuki), strike the enemy's face from above with the right fist and bring the left fist near the chest.

The landing of the feet and the right punch occur at the same time. Movement #57, #58 and #59 are continuous. Try to jump as high as possible - this is a practice for moving the body. When kicking in the air, do not lean the upper body forward. Also, leave no strength inside the crossed arms.

Along with movement #57, do a left and right jodan defense simultaneously. Once movement #57 is completed, immediately execute movement #58. Do not perform the in-air double kick if you have a hold on the opponent. It would be nonsense to

KUSHAN-KU

MOVEMENT #59 (3)

jump, then kick an enemy who is being held. In karate, one tries to not grapple with the opponent; if one is that close, always attack.

MOVEMENT #60 (1)

MOVEMENT #60 (2)

KUSHAN-KU

MOVEMENT #60

Using the right arm, scoop up the opponent's kicking leg, bend slightly forward and using the right foot as a pivot to turn to the right, move the left foot to the right foot's location, lower the left arm, turn around (now facing forward as a start), raise the body firmly and throw the enemy downward. Stop both arms at a position to do a jodan defense, with the palms inward. Extend the left arm as it moves to match the movement of the right arm. When scooping opponent's kicking leg, be sure not to get kicked yourself. When bending, bend the whole body, not just at the waist; keep the body low. Too much strength in the shoulders destabilizes the lower body. Use the strength of the whole body.

KUSHAN-KU

MOVEMENT #61

KUSHAN-KU

MOVEMENT #61

To finish, pull open the right foot slightly, lower both fists with palms open, placing the left above the right and assume the posture for preparation.

Finally, as in Pin-an, pull the feet together left foot first, then the right foot; place the hands in front, apart.

KIRITSU

Finally, as in Pin-an, pull the feet together left foot first, then the right foot; place the hands in front, apart.

ナイハンチ

NAIHANCHI

The "Naihanchi" stance does not exist in Japanese martial arts on its own, yet it is valid and effective. Its constituents are simple, but managing them is difficult. This kata is said sometimes to take more than one lifetime to master completely. Naihanchi has Shodan, Nidan and Sandan, but one only needs to practice the Shodan. This kata has many derivatives as well, depending on who is teaching it.

The Naihanchi which will be illustrated, comes from Ryu Kyu, in Japan and is quite uncommon nowadays. Many in Ryu Kyu do not use it themselves. This is probably because this kata is not really appealing to the eye. However, even nowadays, there are some kata which have certain movements from this one incorporated into them, which probably happened over time.

This Naihanchi was said to have been taught by a Ryu Kyu master, named Kibe Choki. To this, I added and altered slightly. Kibe was relatively conservative; he chose to not alter this kata too much, which is fine. I also believe that this format is the most valid, in my opinion. From "Naihanchi," one may progress to "Sei-shan," and furthermore, to "Chinto," to further master Japanese indigenous martial arts with diligent practice.

HOW TO STAND - NAIHANCHI

Open the legs to about shoulder width and point the toes slightly inward with the body slightly lowered as well; and place both fists (thumbs together, palms inward) between the knee and upper stomach. Keep the upper body in its natural state; do not curve or bend it and "stand" with the whole body, not just the legs. The waist nor the legs are supporting the body; the body is. The body is supporting the body. This "feeling" can only be attained through repeated training, so practice until it is achieved. Anything that feels awkward will become comfortable through repeated practice. What may feel comfortable to the human perception can become uncomfortable over long years of training. Some prefer to sit cross-legged, while others do not. However, it is obvious that if there is tension in the legs, then it would be difficult to move the body, for example. In Naihanchi, one must not place strength unnecessarily in the legs to facilitate a turn or other similar movement.

The waist must be used instead. One important thing to remember is to not collapse the posture of the legs by placing strength in them. This is not "Naihanchi's" stance. It is sometimes called a "jockey's stance" and how appropriate that seems. I do not know much about riding horses, but this stance must be how one rides a horse. One does not rest his body weight on the horse itself, or on his own feet completely. One should imagine being able to turn to the rear suddenly without hindering the horse's activity. Not on yourself, nor on the horse. A strange expression, but very true in this situation.

All hand movements are done high. In this kata, this statement is true. When hands are held high, one concentrates about his hands and his lower body tends to collapse easily. It is with this fact in mind; that one trains Naihanchi without compromising his stance or posture.

POSTURE FOR PREPARATION
As both feet are drawn together, both hands perform as in Kushan-ku. After the kata is complete, do not let your stance falter. One must begin and end with both feet together. Thus, begin with both feet closed together.

NAIHANCHI

MOVEMENT #1 (1)

MOVEMENT #1 (2)

NAIHANCHI

MOVEMENT #1

Do as in Kushan-ku movement #1 and turn both wrists so the left palm covers the right knuckles and the fingertips are lowered slightly, downward. Then quietly move the head to face left, then face right.

To move the face from side to side is both a preparatory exercise as well as a movement to exercise caution to one's sides.

MOVEMENT #1 (5)

NAIHANCHI

MOVEMENT #1 (3)

MOVEMENT #1 (4)

MOVEMENT #1 (6)

MOVEMENT #1 (7)

MOVEMENT #2 (1)

MOVEMENT #2 (2)

NAIHANCHI

MOVEMENT #2
Lower the body slightly and cross the left leg over the right leg and stand on the outer edge of the left foot (same applies for the right foot), then move the right foot to the right and enter into the "Naihanchi stance." This style of walking is called "Chidori." Simultaneously, tense both elbows, then bend them to bring both palms up to the upper chest and with the right shuto, perform a shuto thrusting defense to the right. The extended arm should be below the shoulder, but the defense should occur above the chest. The left fist should be pulled in beside the chest, with the forearm (beneath the left chest) horizontal. The movements of the feet and hands must occur simultaneously. The body must move smoothly; all and every action must occur continuously. In the "Chidori" carry the whole body, not just the legs or the portion above the waist.

NAIHANCHI

MOVEMENT #3

NAIHANCHI

MOVEMENT #3
Twist the upper body to the right and strike with the left elbow.

Remain in a comfortable stance even after twisting the upper body to the right. Do not allow strength to remain in any body parts.

Try to make both shoulders face right and keep both forearms horizontal and below the shoulder (above the chest).

The twisting of the upper body occurs via the waist. All following movements follow this rule.

NAIHANCHI

MOVEMENT #4

NAIHANCHI

MOVEMENT #4
Draw the right fist back to the chest, face the left palm down by moving the forearm and twist the body to the left to face forward; the face should point to the left.

When the upper body is not fully facing forward, the face can not point fully to the left. Be sure to maintain a correct posture. Keep both forearms horizontal and parallel to each other. The face looks left, but the upper body faces straight ahead. For this, place no extra strength anywhere.

NAIHANCHI

MOVEMENT #5

NAIHANCHI

MOVEMENT #5
With the left arm, do a left gedan block.

If only the arms are used, the posture of the upper body and neck will collapse. Execute only when the upper body is fully facing to the left.

NAIHANCHI

MOVEMENT #6

NAIHANCHI

MOVEMENT #6
Punch left diagonally - ahead with the right fist and immediately return the forearm so that it is horizontal in front of the chest (try to keep it as horizontal as possible). Place the left fist at the chest's side.

When punching, make sure the right shoulder does not move forward. Hence, punch with the whole body. Here, the waist is not used. This is a movement to practice punching with the upper body only. The punching arm must have no excessive strength after the punch is thrown. Do not punch thinking about drawing the arm back. The fist will naturally return after contact. For this, leave no extra strength in the punching arm.

MOVEMENT #7 (1)

MOVEMENT #7 (2)

NAIHANCHI

MOVEMENT #7
In that stance, cross the right leg over the left leg and follow with the left leg to do a "Chidori" to the left, then do a naihanchi stance and simultaneously face forward and raise the right forearm to do a right jodan block. The elbow should maintain its level.

Move the body with no excessive motions or movements; high or low. Take care not to do the defense too far to the outside. The outside edge of the right forearm should be "in-line" with the outer edge of the right shoulder. Again, use the whole body for the defense.

NAIHANCHI

MOVEMENT #8

NAIHANCHI

MOVEMENT #8
Do a right gedan-block with the right arm and pull in the left fist beside the chest in preparation to strike upward.

Do not tense the elbow as the right gedan defense is being done (an incomplete gedan-defense will result). The left arm is extended and raised with the elbow drawn in (do not let it cross with the right arm, when crossed, it becomes difficult to move the limbs) beside the chest as the fist is pointed upward.

If only the arms are used here, the knees will tend to bounce, the wrists will bend and the upper body will twist to the left, so use caution.

NAIHANCHI

MOVEMENT #9

NAIHANCHI

MOVEMENT #9
With the left fist, strike the enemy's forehead and nose. Then, immediately do a left jodan defense and place the right forearm horizontally in front of the chest with the palms facing down. It is opposite to Pin-an Godan movement #16, however, hold the stance high.

Do not do the jodan defense with the force of the left arm. If done correctly, the forearm should automatically enter the movements for a defense, on its own.

NAIHANCHI

MOVEMENT #10

NAIHANCHI

MOVEMENT #10
Face left.

Turn the head quickly, to observe any opponents to one's left side.

NAIHANCHI

MOVEMENT #11 (1)

MOVEMENT #11 (2)

NAIHANCHI

MOVEMENT#11

Lift the left lower leg enough to almost be able to see its sole, bring it to the right knee and return it to its origin.

This movement is not a foot sweep. It is a variation of a stance, hence, practice diligently. It must feel no less comfortable than standing normally. The objective here is to see if there is too much strength being placed in the leg itself. Hence, lift the foot as high as possible without straining the leg and return it quickly to its origin. Do not extend the right knee, or put any excessive weight onto the right leg and return to the exact form that was present before the movement was started.

NAIHANCHI

MOVEMENT #12

NAIHANCHI

MOVEMENT #12

Twist the upper body to the left, maintain the stance and do a jodan block with the left forearm.

Block using the whole body's strength and not just the arms. Twist the upper body without destabilizing the lower body. Some people do so, but there is no need to perform this movement and movement #11 continuously.

NAIHANCHI

MOVEMENT #13

NAIHANCHI

MOVEMENT #13
Turn the face completely to the right (face behind one's self).

MOVEMENT #14 (1)

MOVEMENT #14 (2)

NAIHANCHI

MOVEMENT #14

Without altering one's posture significantly, do as in movement #11 with the right leg.

NAIHANCHI

MOVEMENT #15

NAIHANCHI

MOVEMENT #15

Maintain your posture, twist the upper body to the right and do a left jodan defense to the left.

NAIHANCHI

MOVEMENT #16

NAIHANCHI

MOVEMENT #16

Turn the body back to face forward, straight, face left and with palms facing downward, bring the left forearm horizontally to the front of the chest, while simultaneously placing the right fist beside the chest.

While turning the body, do not twist just the upper body to the right, or allow the left shoulder to rise (face forward straight and this movement becomes easier.) Rather than twisting the body, turn it and place no excessive strength in the turn. There is no need for any excessive power here.

NAIHANCHI

MOVEMENT #17

NAIHANCHI

MOVEMENT #17
Without twisting the upper body or the shoulders, punch both fists towards the left side, horizontally.

Do not push the right shoulder forward (maintain the body to face forward) and extend the right arm as far as possible. Be careful not to twist the body to the right, or lean forward / backwards to the right. Remember to punch with the whole body. Never punch with the strength of the arms alone. One must punch high without lowering the right elbow or leaning the body.

NAIHANCHI

MOVEMENT #18

NAIHANCHI

MOVEMENT #18
Turn the left wrist / forearm to grasp the opponent's attack (palms facing up - the opponent's palm as well) by his knuckles (if he uses his right arm) and while nullifying his attack, pull in the right fist towards the chest.

Perform this movement unhurriedly, yet strongly and assertively. Use the whole body; not just the arm's strength, or else your body will twist and your shoulders will move. Leave no excessive strength after pulling the right arm.

NAIHANCHI

MOVEMENT #19

MOVEMENT #20

NAIHANCHI

MOVEMENT #19 - #33
For movement #19 to 33, do as in movement #3 to #17 in the opposite direction.

NAIHANCHI

MOVEMENT #21

MOVEMENT #22

MOVEMENT #24

MOVEMENT #25

MOVEMENT #23 (1)

MOVEMENT #23 (2)

MOVEMENT #26

MOVEMENT #27 (1)

MOVEMENT #27 (2)

MOVEMENT #28

MOVEMENT #30 (2)

MOVEMENT #31

MOVEMENT #29

MOVEMENT #30 (1)

MOVEMENT #32

MOVEMENT #33

NAIHANCHI

MOVEMENT #34

NAIHANCHI

MOVEMENT #34
Quietly draw the right foot back, face forward, lower both fists opened and assume the posture for preparation.

Although one is about to finish, always be prepared to defend from an enemy's attack.

End with the separation of both hands and toes from each other and assuming the posture as at start.

This kata focuses on movement - fundamental movements and variations of these according to the situation.

These movements involve the usage of the body's full strength in the former and swift, quick movements with respect to the latter. In the former, distribute the body's strength equally,

without becoming too tense to keep a smooth "flow" of movements. Keep in mind that all movements occur using the whole body - never the legs or arms by themselves. The fundamentals practiced in the former are then quickly executed; altered, if necessary.

When training with this kata, remember to be able to react in any direction at any time.

セイシャン

SEI-SHAN

This kata focuses on movement, fundamental movements and variations of these according to the situation. These movements involve the usage of the body's full strength in the former and swift, quick movements with respect to the latter. In the former, distribute the body's stength equally, without becoming too tense to keep a smooth "flow" of movements.

Keep in mind that all movements occur using the whole body, never the legs or arms by themselves. What fundamentals practiced in the former are then quickly executed; altered, if necessary.

When training with kata, remember to be able to react in any direction at any time.

SEI-SHAN

SEI-SHAN - STANCE

Keep the distance between the feet minimal, but keep the toes comfortably ahead of the heels in this stance; also, lower the body slightly.

SEI-SHAN

POSTURE FOR PREPARATION

Identical to that used in Pin-an.

SEI-SHAN

MOVEMENT #1

SEI-SHAN

MOVEMENT #1
With the body lowered, slightly turn the left foot inward and move it forward from the inside to the outside; turn the right ankle outward and move the right forearm upward (palm facing up) and the left forearm down (palm facing down), then cross them and pull the right fist beside the waist and raise the left forearm to do a Chudan defense from the inside towards the outside.

Do not shift one's body weight on to the right leg then move the left leg. The thighs must help in this, to move smoothly. Move as if to draw an arc with the thigh, to the outer side.

When moving both arms, one may practice doing this by placing strength in the lower abdomen. Then do the defense at mid-level and hold the fist relatively low. The left fist should be at chest's height. Be careful not to adhere the left elbow to the body as this is done.

Do not think of the legs' motions too much, lest the defense becomes incomplete and vice versa. Do not place too much strength in the shoulders as the defense is being done. Do this movement with strength placed in the lower abdomen. Do not allow the right elbow to rise from the body. Start practice by placing strength in the stomach, then the whole body. This is especially important in Sei-shan, proper muscles must be used. Hence develop strength in the proper muscles as well. Thus, use the whole body for each movement. Do not place or use strength mistakingly. Be careful.

SEI-SHAN

MOVEMENT #2

SEI-SHAN

MOVEMENT #2

Do a right punch and place the left fist beside the chest.

The right should strike at the level of the lower abdomen. Do not allow the elbow to rise as contact is being made. Use the movement of the left fist to balance the right punch.

SEI-SHAN

MOVEMENT #3

SEI-SHAN

MOVEMENT #3
Turn the left leg inward slightly (almost twisted slightly), move the right leg forward as in movement #1, bend the right forearm (palm facing down) almost diagonally and move it to the left lower abdomen and as the foot's stance is completed, erect the right forearm to do a Chudan defense as the left arm did in movement #1.

When moving forward, do not place the body's weight on the left foot; rather, move the upper body as it faces forward and "carry" the right leg entirely - then naturally, the right leg will be able to draw an "arc" as it advances forward. As in Naihanchi, move forward with the body and assume the proper stance using both the legs and the wrist. While defending, be careful not to twist the upper body - this will cause the elbow to come into contact with the body.

SEI-SHAN

MOVEMENT #4

SEI-SHAN

MOVEMENT #4
Do a left punch and pull in the right fist, as in movement #2.

SEI-SHAN

MOVEMENT #5

SEI-SHAN

MOVEMENT #5
Do as in movement #3 - advance the left foot forward and do a left defense.

SEI-SHAN

MOVEMENT #6

SEI-SHAN

MOVEMENT #6
Do a right punch and pull in the left fist.

SEI-SHAN

MOVEMENT #7

SEI-SHAN

MOVEMENT #7
Extend the index fingers of both fists, point both palms downward and raise both hands to just above the chest level (both fingertips are slightly apart) while simultaneously raising both elbows.

This movement is the basics to and of, defending with the elbows. Be careful not to raise both fists too high and maintain strength in the lower abdomen.

SEI-SHAN

MOVEMENT #8

SEI-SHAN

MOVEMENT #8
Strike forward with both fists (so that they are almost touching) together.

Do not allow the shoulders or the elbows to rise in this movement. Keep both elbows low and strike low (enemy's lower abdomen) with placed strength first in the stomach, then distributed evenly throughout the body,

Do not tense the elbows. Also, do not lower the fists, then strike; lower them as they strike.

SEI-SHAN

MOVEMENT #9 (1)

MOVEMENT #9 (2)

SEI-SHAN

MOVEMENT #9

With both hands in shuto, twist the forearms (both palms facing each other) and do a jodan defense simultaneously. Both elbows should be lower than the shoulders and the forearms should be held vertical.

As the defense is done with both elbows held high, be careful to not just raise both arms, or to not fully twist the forearms (so the palms do not face each other). Both palms must face each other fully and both defenses must occur simultaneously. Because the elbows are located high, make sure to defend an attack and not just "lift" the attack from below. Both hands are maintained in shuto form.

SEI-SHAN

MOVEMENT #10 (1)

MOVEMENT #10 (2)

SEI-SHAN

MOVEMENT #10
With both forearms, do a gedan block forward, towards both sides.

Be careful to not just lower both arms, but do not lower and block with them. Be "lively" and do the block accurately.

SEI-SHAN

MOVEMENT#11 (1)

SEI-SHAN

MOVEMENT#11

Bring the right foot over the left foot diagonally left forward, turn left to face the rear and take a left Sei-shan stance. As the feet take their respective places, simultaneously do a left shuto gedan block and a right shuto Chudan block. The right shuto should be held so that the palm is horizontal and defends from the opponent's attack.

The body carries the feet and the whole body must rotate. Turn the left arm outward (or else the elbow will rise) to face the palm upward and bring the small finger to the upper part of the right arm; and with the right arm slightly extended, turn the forearm inward and bring below the left forearm / elbow to cross them (the right palm faces diagonally down and forward, in front of the left lower stomach) and as the feet take their stance, both defenses occur at the same time.

MOVEMENT #11 (2)

This movement is difficult; one tends to do this using the forearms alone. The right defense, I think, needs to be practiced repeatedly. There is also a tendency to place the right elbow to the body and twist the upper body towards the right. Twist the left forearm fully and raise the right forearm as it is being twisted, to defend properly to the side.

SEI-SHAN

MOVEMENT #12

SEI-SHAN

MOVEMENT #12

Pull back the right arm and flip the palm over using the wrist and with that hand, grasp the opponent's wrist and pull towards one's self.

This movement is very difficult to describe in words, so I can only suggest practice. This is similar to the "kote" technique in jui jitsu. The right elbow draws back along the chest. Defend from the enemy's attack and as the palm is flipping over, move it along the enemy's forearm to grasp his wrist and pull towards one's self. When pulling, do not raise the elbow and pull slightly downward. When pulling on the opponent's wrist, pull so that the line of his attacking arm is in line to that of your pulling motion - that is, vertically straight. The point in contact with the opponent should move the same distance that one's elbow moves. If one flips the palm over too quickly, this will cause the wrist to rotate and will not allow the collapse of the enemy's stance. This is one of the difficult movements, due to the difficulty of these actions.

When there is too much power in the right shoulder, it will prevent you from gaining a good grip of the opponent's wrist, because the elbow will rise. The hand should be held slightly higher than the elbow and do not bend the wrist. When pulling (left arm as well), distribute the body's strength evenly.

Experiment and practice.

SEI-SHAN

MOVEMENT #13

SEI-SHAN

MOVEMENT #13

Relax the body momentarily, advance the right foot as in movement #3 and cross both shuto as in movement #11 and do a right gedan defense and a left Chudan defense simultaneously, as in movement #11.

SEI-SHAN

MOVEMENT #14

SEI-SHAN

MOVEMENT #14
Do as in movement #12 to the left.

SEI-SHAN

MOVEMENT #15

SEI-SHAN

MOVEMENT #15
Advance the left foot forward and do as in movement #11.

SEI-SHAN

MOVEMENT #16

SEI-SHAN

MOVEMENT #16
Do as in movement #12.

Every movement up to movement #16 are fundamental movements and focus upon the controlling and moving of the body. Essentially, perform each movement silently and with strength being evenly distributed throughout the whole body.

From movement #17, it is essential that each movement be performed swiftly - each movement shall be a variation of this stance. Later, Shimata-tachi and the T-stance will be combined to freely incorporate changes into this stance.

SEI-SHAN

MOVEMENT #17

SEI-SHAN

MOVEMENT #17
Move the right foot forward to the right, followed by the left foot, skipping slightly and do a Sei-shan stance while doing a right jodan defense at the same time. Bring the left fist beside the chest.

The stance is a variation of the fundamentals shown earlier; keep the space between the left and right feet small. Stand so that the inner heel of the hind (left) foot is in line with the thumb toe of the front (right) foot. Leave the left foot as is and pull back the right foot as one faces the enemy. Practicing in this stance facilitates any later variations of movement.

Take a comfortable stance. One must be able to take this stance without thinking about it too much.

SEI-SHAN

MOVEMENT #18 (1)

MOVEMENT #18 (2)

SEI-SHAN

MOVEMENT #18
Do a left, then right, punch.

Movement #17 and #18 are continuous.

SEI-SHAN

MOVEMENT # 19

SEI-SHAN

MOVEMENT # 19
Turn around to the left and rear, advance and do a left jodan defense.

The stance is similar to movement #17.

MOVEMENT #20 (1)

MOVEMENT #20 (2)

SEI-SHAN

MOVEMENT #20
Do a right, then left, punch.

Movement #19 and #20 are continuous.

SEI-SHAN

MOVEMENT #21

SEI-SHAN

MOVEMENT #21
Advance towards the right and do as in movement #17.

MOVEMENT #22 (1)

MOVEMENT #22 (2)

SEI-SHAN

MOVEMENT #22
Same as movement #18

Movement #21 and #22 occur continuously.

SEI-SHAN

MOVEMENT #23 (1)

SEI-SHAN

MOVEMENT #23

Avoid an enemy's kick from the rear and pull the left leg back while preparing to do a front kick to the enemy in front; simultaneously, use the backside of the left fist to strike the nose of the enemy in front upward, bring the fist above the head and place the right fist beside the chest. Turn the body to the left and simultaneously step down on the hind enemy's kicking leg with the left backside of the left fist. The body should be sideways, to place both enemies to the left and right, with a Shimata-tachi stance.

Face left and look to the hind enemy to be in front and rear and in response to a kick from the rear, pull in the left leg as if to kick the enemy in front while striking the enemy's nose upward and as one turns the other way step down on the enemy's left leg with the left leg, while striking downward on the opponent's face with the backside of the left fist.

SEI-SHAN

MOVEMENT #23 (2)

The main focus is placed on switching stances to the Shimata-tachi. When stepping down with the left, do not lose balance in the Shimata-tachi. Use the right heel as a pivot so the right toe can turn inward slightly.

When striking upward with the left fist, extend fully and execute firmly and swiftly, balanced by the movement of the right fist. When both these movements are executed, the left fist should naturally stop near the top of the head and the body should turn more easily. Take care in the movement of the left fist, as it can cause the body to lean, or the foot to rise, or make an incomplete Shimata-tachi stance.

This movement is difficult due to all its constituent movements. The left hand's movement is very important here. When using the left fist, remember to balance that action with the pulling in of the right fist. Practice accurately and sufficiently.

MOVEMENT #24 (1)

MOVEMENT #24 (2)

SEI-SHAN

MOVEMENT #24

Imagine that the enemy pulls you in by grabbing your left arm; do a "Chidon" with the right foot and follow through with the body in the pulled direction and do a left side kick; at the same time, pull the left arm firmly back beside the chest and as the kicking left foot is lowered, attack low with the left fist. The feet form the letter "T" and the body is in a posture to punch. Remember to switch from a Shimata-tachi to a letter "T" stance.

MOVEMENT #24 (3)

SEI-SHAN

MOVEMENT #25

SEI-SHAN

MOVEMENT #25
Assume the "Uchiwa" stance and twist the upper body to the left and do a right gyaku-tsuki; return the left fist to the chest and turn the upper body back.

The stance changes, as in movement #19.

When moving the feet, take care not to punch using the arm's strength only, but do incorporate the waist into the punch. Take a stance as in movement #17. But do not move with the legs only. Move the whole body, stand naturally and strike with help from the twist of the waist.

SEI-SHAN

MOVEMENT #26

SEI-SHAN

MOVEMENT #26
With the same posture, do a left jodan defense and bring the right fist back to the chest.

MOVEMENT #27 (1)

MOVEMENT #27 (2)

SEI-SHAN

MOVEMENT #27
Perform movement #23 to the right.

MOVEMENT #28 (1)

MOVEMENT #28 (2)

SEI-SHAN

MOVEMENT #28

Perform movement #24 to the right.

MOVEMENT #28 (3)

SEI-SHAN

MOVEMENT #29

SEI-SHAN

MOVEMENT #29
As in movement #25, do a left punch and place the right fist beside the chest.

SEI-SHAN

MOVEMENT #30

SEI-SHAN

MOVEMENT #30
In the same posture, do a right jodan defense and bring the left fist beside the chest.

MOVEMENT #31 (1)

MOVEMENT #31 (2)

SEI-SHAN

MOVEMENT #31
Identical to movement #23.

SEI-SHAN

MOVEMENT #32 (1)

MOVEMENT #32 (2)

SEI-SHAN

MOVEMENT #32
To kick the enemy's arm with the right foot, face the left palm toward the right toe with the small finger side downward and kick in an arc (called a "Mikazuki" kick "crescent" kick); then pull the kicking leg back and do the stance as in movement #25 and as the stance is completed, twist the waist to punch towards the left with the right fist. Bring the left fist beside the chest.

When kicking with the right foot, open the left toe outward slightly. Do this kick in a comfortable position. However, the main focus of this movement is the switching of stance styles, not the kick.

Perform every action by using the whole body and it should be not so difficult to execute.

SEI-SHAN

MOVEMENT #33 (1)

SEI-SHAN

MOVEMENT #33
Leave the right foot as it is, pull in the left foot and cover the right leg with the left inner thigh and stand on the left toe; simultaneously, bend all five fingers so that the inner sides all almost touch the palm and bend the thumb backwards to line up with the palm as well; bend the right elbow slightly and as the body is lowered, thrust downward, both arms together, to do a gedan defense. Both wrists are touching; defend with the lower areas of both palms.

Keep the upper body straight and do not look at the hands. All movements must occur in one movement. Pull the left leg with the whole body and twist the waist to the right to defend from an enemy's kick. Extend both elbows for the gedan defense and block the kicking foot in front of both arms.

SEI-SHAN

MOVEMENT #33 (2)

When pulling the left leg, the leg, the body and the twisting of the waist must occur all at once, while twisting the left heel outward and placing the left leg so that the left knee covers above the right knee, in contact - lower the body as well. The body will stabilize if the body's weight rests at the knees. This movement allows one to avoid quick footsweeps or other attacks of the enemy's leg.

SEI-SHAN

MOVEMENT #34

SEI-SHAN

MOVEMENT #34
Do not move the right leg; but move the left leg to return to the posture for preparation.

Watch how the right toe is pointed after assuming the posture for preparation. Practice so that the stance is not too wide open. Do not move on the legs' strength alone. Finishing stance is the same as in Pin-an.

Sei-shan does not exist on its own in Japanese martial art. This is hardly used in many cases. This is probably due to a lack of training and an incomplete understanding of meanings and objectives of the movements. Although quite difficult, they are quite essential. Take sufficient care, practice and studying. I do not know why some movements occur swiftly, while others occur slowly. Movement #23, #27 and #31 are often done

slowly; probably to allow one to recover from any fatigue. However, let that not be so.

チントウ

CHINTO

KIRITSU

It is better to practice "Chinto" after practicing Pin-an and Sei-shan first. This kata does incorporate some characteristics of those, in actual practice.

Start at Pin-an, the Kushanku, Naihanchi, Sei-shan and finally, on to Chinto.

POSTURE FOR PREPARATION
Identical to that in Pin-an.

CHINTO

MOVEMENT #1

CHINTO

MOVEMENT #1

Place the right foot behind the left foot, lower the body and face it to the right, almost Mahanmi and with the right palm and the left fist's backside, do a jodan defense simultaneously. Point the head straight ahead, at the enemy in front.

Although both hands move together, these are two separate blocks, as in Pin-an Godan, movement #9, jodan defense; hence, do not attach the two hands together firmly. The right thumb should not exceed the palm (place the thumb against the index finger firmly). Both hands are kept vertical in order to completely defend from the enemy's attack. Do not place strength in the shoulders, this will make the defense incomplete and weak. Place both hands so that the left thumb and the right small finger almost touch, do not let the upper body twist to the left.

CHINTO

MOVEMENT #2

CHINTO

MOVEMENT #2
Turn the right forearm outward and lower the left forearm to mid-level (right arm below, palm facing up; left arm above, palm facing down), and defend against any attacks to the left side of the body.

As in Pin-an Godan, movement #10, both forearms are horizontal and only slightly making contact. Here, the left side of the body remains wide open for attack after both forearms are lowered in front of the stomach; so use caution.

CHINTO

MOVEMENT #3

CHINTO

MOVEMENT #3
In the same posture, do a left punch and bring the right fist to the chest.

Hold the waist firmly to not allow the de-stabilization of the body and pull the right fist back firmly.

CHINTO

MOVEMENT #4

CHINTO

MOVEMENT #4
Twist the waist to the left and do a right gyaku-tsuki while placing the left fist at the chest and place the feet as they are in Sei-shan, movement #25. Movement #1 to movement #4 are continuous.

Rotate the right heel outward and stand as in Sei-shan, movement #17 and punch with the twist of the waist. Do not open both feet excessively to the sides, or the objective of the Sei-shan stance is nullified.

CHINTO

MOVEMENT #5

CHINTO

MOVEMENT #5
Move the right leg in front of the left leg and turn around full circle to the left and assume the Shimata-tachi stance, while at the same time doing a right gedan block to the right. The face is turned to the right. Withdraw the right leg in response to a kick from the hind enemy, turn and take Mahanmi Shimata-tachi to the hind enemy and follow with a block of the attack to the lower abdomen.

Do not move with the legs alone. Move and turn with the whole body. Do not swing the right arm too much in doing the gedan block. With the right fist near the right ear, twisting the forearm while bending the elbow, the fist should travel a straight course (right palm facing backwards), in doing the gedan block.

CHINTO

MOVEMENT #6

CHINTO

MOVEMENT #6
Turn left (front originally) and with both shuto, do a jodan defense as in Pin-an Godan, movement #9.

Turn completely to the left. One must not turn just the upper body. Move as if to quickly respond to an enemy at left. If both feet are not stable, then the same can be said for the body which rests on those feet and an unstable posture will result.

CHINTO

MOVEMENT #7

CHINTO

MOVEMENT #7
Form fists with both shuto and do a Chudan uchi-otoshi defense to the left and right simultaneously (small fingers pointed downward).

(Refer to Kushan-ku, movement #58.)

CHINTO

MOVEMENT #8 (1)

MOVEMENT #8 (2)

CHINTO

MOVEMENT #8

Placing both fists by the chest, do a jumping double-kick and as in Pin-an Yondan, movement #3, do a gedan defense to the left and right simultaneously.

Movement #6, #7 and #8 occur continuously.

MOVEMENT #8 (3)

MOVEMENT #9

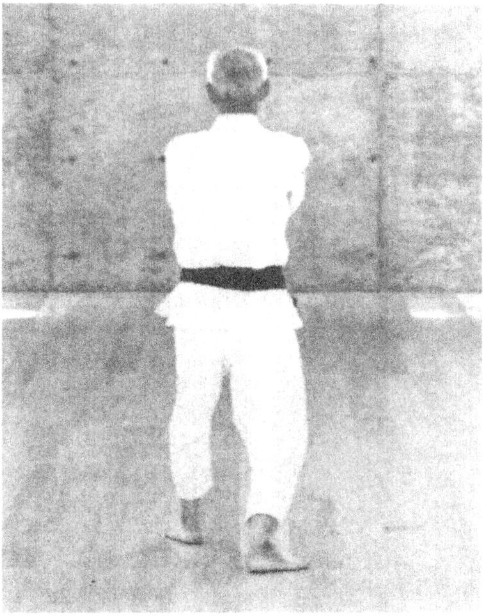

CHINTO

MOVEMENT #9
Place both fists at the chest and using the right foot as a pivot, turn right and place the left foot to the rear and do a gedan defense, as in movement #8.

CHINTO

MOVEMENT #10

CHINTO

MOVEMENT #10
Do as in Pin-an Godan, movement #17. Lean the body down toward the left in response to a high attack from behind (an enemy's staff) and place the right fist on the lower right side of the body and the left fist at the chest (right palm facing down, left palm facing up). The face turns right.

Move with the same reasoning as in Pin-an Godan, movement #17.

CHINTO

MOVEMENT#11

CHINTO

MOVEMENT#11
Move the left leg to the right and in the same direction, lean the body to the right, downward. With shuto, the left is placed low (palms facing down) and the right in front of the chest (palm facing upward). The body faces to the opposite.

In practice, erect the body fully before moving the body. This is to practice leaning the body against the enemy's jodan attack.

CHINTO

MOVEMENT #12

CHINTO

MOVEMENT #12
Step forward with the right foot and with both shuto, do a jodan defense to each side simultaneously. Keep both arms at shoulder width. Both shuto jodan defense cross with the right on the inside and the left on the outside with both palms inward (facing the body), while they are raised, with both forearms being turned from inside to outside as they do the block. Take care not to raise the elbows, or put strength in the arms.

In Chinto, this defense must be done quickly, yet effectively. The defense must complement the shift in the body's posture. Also the actions to the left and to the right must be executed at the same time, lest following movements may suffer. Originally, this was probably not the case, but it is now so due to time, erred transmission of movement and simply - mistakes.

CHINTO

MOVEMENT #13

CHINTO

MOVEMENT #13
Turn to the left by moving the left foot and assume the Shimata-tachi (the stance is narrower than a normal Shimata-tachi) and with both shuto, do a jodan defense simultaneously. Keep both arms at shoulder width. Cross the right forearm to the outside of the left forearm.

In controlling these movements, use the cautionary notes I have used for previous movements.

CHINTO

MOVEMENT #14

CHINTO

MOVEMENT #14
Place both hands into fists and lower them to the front; extend both knees and face towards the left, as in the posture for preparation. Do this silently. This prepares one for the next movement.

CHINTO

MOVEMENT #15

CHINTO

MOVEMENT #15

Open the right leg outward and lean the body to the right and do as in Pin-an Godan, movement #20.

MOVEMENT #16 (1)

MOVEMENT #16 (2)

CHINTO

MOVEMENT #16
Bring the right leg to the left, turn left and face the opposite direction and lean the body as in Pin-an Godan movement #21. The head is facing the same direction and should be looking right.

This movement is a continuous movement from left to right, so remember to face the body straight forward before movement.

MOVEMENT #17 (1)

MOVEMENT #17 (2)

CHINTO

MOVEMENT #17

Imagine enemies to the sides and turn the body backwards (right leg as pivot, turn left), and bring the left leg to the right leg (use the whole body to move the leg), erect the body upright (as if to pull in and avoid the enemy's attack), look at the enemy to the left and instantaneously turn the body left and face the body to the enemy at the right, lean right and avoid his jodan attack. The body faces opposite in comparison to movement #16 and the face is turned to the left. (Same as movement #15.)

CHINTO

MOVEMENT #18

CHINTO

MOVEMENT #18
Turn the head straight forward, (do not look down), bring the right leg directly behind the left leg and stand on the right toes while lowering the body and with both hands in a fist, do a Gedan defense forward with both arms together. Cross the arms with the right arm above the left and keep the upper body straight. Do not place all the body's weight on the left leg alone.

CHINTO

MOVEMENT #19

CHINTO

MOVEMENT #19
Do a Shimata-tachi by moving the right leg to the right (not too much space between the feet) and lower the body slightly. Do a jodan defense to the left and right simultaneously. The fists should be in a shuto, as in movement #13.

CHINTO

MOVEMENT #20

CHINTO

MOVEMENT #20
Lower both fists to the front of the body and extend both knees.

CHINTO

MOVEMENT #21

CHINTO

MOVEMENT #21
Place both fists at the waist, as in Pin-an movement #12.

CHINTO

MOVEMENT #22

CHINTO

MOVEMENT #22
As in Pin-an Sandan, movement #13, lower the body while twisting at the waist to the left and turn to the left, while using the right elbow to defend a Chudan attack from the front.

MOVEMENT #23

CHINTO

MOVEMENT #23
Turn the body to the right and do a defense with the left elbow. Movement #22 and #23 are done while the head is turned forward.

CHINTO

MOVEMENT #24

CHINTO

MOVEMENT #24

With the right leg as a pivot, turn right and face to the rear; bring the left foot behind the right foot and stand on the toes (same stance as in Pin-an Godan, movement #16), and do a jodan defense to the left and right as in movement #19.

CHINTO

MOVEMENT #25 (1)

MOVEMENT #25 (2)

CHINTO

MOVEMENT #25
Turn to the left and raise the left leg, bend the knee and place the foot near the right knee, touching slightly, place the left arm low to the left, right arm high to the right, then place both fists beside the right chest as in Pin-an Yondan, movement #5 (do not place the right fist on top of the left fist). As a block is done with the left fist to the enemy's Chudan attack, do a left side, kick as in Pin-an Yondan, movement #6. Step forward left with the right foot, do a right jun-tsuki and bring the left fist beside the chest.

When pulling the leg back, use the movement of both arms to stablilize the body and then place them, quickly, by the chest in one, continuous movement. One must move quickly, but perform each and every movement fully. The left fist may strike in any direction to the side, however, to keep the body stable,

MOVEMENT #25 (3)

MOVEMENT #25 (4)

one should aim for the enemy's abdomen.

One should be especially cautious as the foot is placed near the knee of the standing leg, as the body can lose its balance easily. The bent leg's knee should only touch the standing leg slightly. Assume this posture as if to kick an enemy. Remember to create an opportunity to attack as one defends from the enemy.

Always be prepared to attack, or counter-attack in any movement, or at any time. Do not pull the leg with the strength of the legs alone. If one thinks of countering an enemy's attack, the pulled leg will naturally assume a position with which to kick. Keep in mind that every movement must be "alive" in kata.

CHINTO

MOVEMENT #26 (1)

MOVEMENT #26 (2)

CHINTO

MOVEMENT #26

Do the stance in movement #25 to the opposite direction, followed by the movements of movement #25 and assume a Sei-shan stance as the kicking leg is lowered; twist the waist to the right and do a left gyaku-tsuki and place the right fist beside the chest.

MOVEMENT #26 (3)

MOVEMENT #26 (4)

MOVEMENT #27 (1)

MOVEMENT #27 (2)

CHINTO

MOVEMENT #27

Turn the body to the left, pull back the left leg and do the opposite movements of movement #26. Take a Sei-shan stance, turn the waist to the left and do a right gyaku-tsuki as before.

CHINTO

MOVEMENT #27 (3)

MOVEMENT #27 (4)

CHINTO

MOVEMENT #28

CHINTO

MOVEMENT #28

Turn the body right, do a Shimata-tachi and in a Mahanmi stance, block the Chudan attack from the rear (similar to the jodan defense as seen in Pin-an Yondan, as the body is turned to the left).

An incomplete defense will result if the right shoulder is made tense, the elbow will rise. Keep the elbow low, block to the side and bend the right wrist as if to grab something.

CHINTO

MOVEMENT #29

CHINTO

MOVEMENT #29
Turn the right foot slightly to the right, do a Sei-shan stance, turn the waist to the right and strike with the left elbow.

Movement #28 and #29 are continuous. When striking with the elbow, keep the forearm vertical and straight. The palm faces inward.

CHINTO

MOVEMENT #30

CHINTO

MOVEMENT #30
Form a left shuto and place it near the left side of the waist with the palm forward and fingertips down, the right fist should be placed at the left palm touching slightly with knuckles downward (do not press into the palm, or grasp the right fist with the left palm).

MOVEMENT #31 (1)

MOVEMENT #31 (2)

CHINTO

MOVEMENT #31

Imagine the enemies to be in front and rear, pull the left leg in to seem like one is about to kick the enemy in front and place it at the right knee (as in movement #25 and on), while striking upward with the right fist at the enemy's nose, place the left shuto at the chest and using the right leg as a pivot, turn to the right (so that one is at a left Mahanmi position to the enemy at rear), placing both fists at the right chest (as in movement #25 and on), followed by a left kick and a left side punch, step forward one step, punch with the right fist and placing the left fist beside the chest.

One will not be able to turn around smoothly if the left shuto is raised along with the right fist, because the body will rise and the stance will be weakened. Strike with the right fist and hold the left shuto at the chest.

MOVEMENT #31 (3)

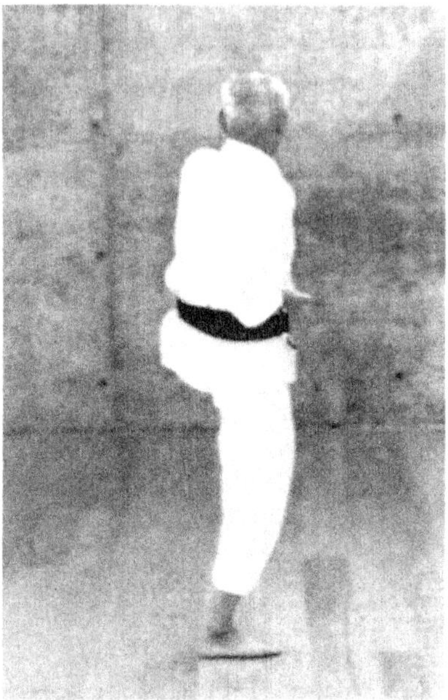

MOVEMENT #31 (4)

CHINTO

MOVEMENT #32

CHINTO

MOVEMENT #32
With the right leg as a pivot, turn to the rear and return the left leg to its starting position, lower both arms and assume the posture for preparation.

Finish as one would with Pin-an.

Karate Do Volume 1 *(Not For Sale)*

Published in 45th Year of the Showa Era, August 25th

Author: Otsuka Hironori

Tokyo, Nerima-ward, Sakura-dai 2-48

Publisher: The Support Group for Otsuka Hironori, Supreme Instructor

Tokyo, Chiyoda-ward, Fujimi 1-9-20
Japanese University of Dentistry
Department of Medical Studies
Heiji Maizumi, Chairperson

Pulished by: Tōyō Publishing　　*Pressing by: Misuba Press*

空　手　道　第一巻　非売品

昭和45年8月25日発行

著者　大塚博紀

東京都練馬区桜台2—48

発行者　大塚博紀最高師範後援会

東京都千代田区富士見1—9—20

日本歯科大学薬理学教室

会長　真泉平治

印刷　東洋印刷　　製版　三葉製版

Printed in Great Britain
by Amazon

79942378R00203